Starting your own business

a Consumer Publication

Consumers' Association
publishers of **Which?**
14 Buckingham Street
London WC2N 6DS

a Consumer Publication

edited by Edith Rudinger

published by Consumers' Association
publishers of **Which?**

Consumer Publications
are available from
Consumers' Association
and from booksellers.
Details are given at
the end of this book.

© Consumers' Association

ISBN 0 85202 236 0
and 0 340 32090 7

 Printed in Great Britain by
Page Bros (Norwich) Ltd

Contents

Foreword

The starting point of this book is a Consumer Publication *Earning money at home* which we published in 1979; ***Starting your own business*** is a logical step from earning money at home, and some of the advice of the previous book applies to this one, too.

Your own business must support you and therefore demands a greater commitment, both psychological and financial, and more courage because of the greater investment and greater risk of failure. Many people have succeeded, through hard work, perhaps helped by luck. Experience, of course, helps – but even without, many people have leapt into the unknown and landed on their feet.

Unconventional businesses often arise from a person noticing a gap and being willing and able to fill it: the young man who would deliver a single flower to an address in the neighbourhood (now a thriving gift service) the dentist who invented a single-tooth toothbrush (at first made by his wife and technician, now a nationwide enterprise), the travel agent's clerk who bought one secondhand bus and whose coach tours are now a household name; the man who invented the better mouse-trap.

You or some member of your family may have said before now 'I wish there were a . . .', or 'if only somebody would do . . . this, that, or the other'. Maybe that is the gap for you to fill.

Whatever business you are thinking of starting, there is a lot to be learned, and a lot of general and specialist information to be gathered. Start with this book.

P.S.

Throughout the book, for he read he or she, and vice versa, for him and his, read her and hers, and so on (except for the bit about maternity leave).

Having what it takes

To run your own business, of whatever kind, you need not only some capital and some capability but also a certain flair, toughness and some good fortune. Just a very few of the people who start out as small businessmen have enough of both flair and luck to end up as millionaires. You might be one of them; more probably you will succeed in making a comfortable living, while enjoying the satisfaction of independence and of doing work you have chosen for yourself.

To achieve this, you must be committed; you must choose a business project that is right for you; and you must prepare yourself as thoroughly as possible for the plunge, before you take it.

commitment

It is no use being half-hearted when starting up a business: you should be motivated positively, not just negatively by a dislike of the job you are in. Your incentive should be to a large extent financial, and do not set your sights too low: from the start, your aim should be to make a reasonable living. If all you want is to supplement a pension, you may find that you do not manage even this much.

In becoming your own boss, you may find yourself working for a harder taskmaster than any you have had, one who offers unlimited working hours, uncertain holidays, and perhaps, to start with, less money than you were earning before. You will be exchanging the support and companionship of fellow workers for a kind of isolation in which you stand or fall by your own decisions.

There will be few executive perks, or none: you will look at these with a different eye when they have to be paid for out of your profits.

The members of your family should feel equally committed. Their moral support, quite apart from any work-support, will be invaluable, especially during periods of difficulty and discouragement. They ought to be aware that their security depends on your success, that you may have less time for family life, and that the rewards may be some time in coming.

choosing your project

Anyone wanting to start a business has either found a product to manufacture or an idea for one, or has decided to go into distribution, or to provide a service. It is unlikely that he will say to himself 'I want to go into business but I don't know whether to be a manufacturer or a distributor or someone providing a service'.

Your choice of business project is a decision you alone can make, because you are in the best position to know what your marketable skills and capabilities are, and which of them you want to be the foundation of your new career.

You may want to capitalise on the knowledge of a trade, the business training or the managerial experience acquired in your previous work. But if it is work that you are unhappy in, you may want to strike out in a new direction.

A hobby which has made you an expert at some trade – for instance, cabinet-making, cooking, dressmaking – can be the start of a business, especially if you have already begun to make money by it in your spare time: you will then have the beginnings of a client list, and some idea of a potential market. When you approach a bank or other organisation for a loan, you will inspire more confidence if you already have some history of successful trading. But remember that it is a big jump from moonlighting to making a living from it, and selling a hobby-item to a few friends and relatives may not be a good indication of its appeal to the general public or of its economic viability.

You may have an original business idea. Perhaps you have designed a new product that fills a gap in the market which everyone else has failed to notice; or you may have an idea for a service which would facilitate the workings of some industry.

You may want to enter an established trade by buying a franchise or into a partnership, or by taking over a going concern. But if the trade is new to you, be wary: you are unlikely to be able to master it at the same time as learning the complexities of running a business. Bear in mind that you will be competing with people who are already established experts in the field. You had better get your training and experience first, by working in the trade for a period, and attending any relevant training courses.

some ways into your own business

If you have developed an original business idea but do not want to deal with the whole of the business side yourself, you may make an agreement with a manufacturer to make your product, retaining for yourself any part of the operation to which you can offer a unique contribution, such as design or marketing. Do not forget that you should, if possible, protect any truly novel idea of yours (for instance, by applying for patent), before disclosing it to any interested party.

Look around to see if you can find any other small firms, old or new, working in the same or a related field, who might be willing to pool resources with you. For instance, a successful 'merger' of this kind has been achieved between the makers of four-poster beds, piano stools and wooden toys respectively: as well as sharing expenses, they were able to develop a common advertising and marketing policy, while remaining autonomous in other ways.

To set up such an arrangement you may have to do a good bit of research to find other firms in your line of trade in your district. Consult your local council and Chamber of Commerce or Chamber of Trade; if there is a Small Business Club, it will probably be willing to advertise your needs among its members. In London, the London Enterprise ▲ Agency, 69 Cannon Street, London EC4N 5AB (telephone: 01-236 2676 or 01-248 4444) runs a 'marriage bureau' to introduce people and firms who need each others' skills and resources.

partial buy-outs

If you have been made redundant by the winding up of a company, consider whether there is any part of the operation or assets (some of the workshop plant, for instance) that you could buy and use in starting a project of your own.

A complete buy-out is a different matter: unless you know exactly why the original company went out of business, and have definite proposals for putting things right, you will not find it eay to raise the necessary finance.

There is nothing to stop employees who leave an existing company from setting up in competition provided they have given no undertaking to the contrary. For instance, there may be a clause in their contract of employment restricting their future business ventures. In any event, the ex-employer may stop former employees from making use of his trade secrets or confidential information by taking out an injunction.

In making your final choice of project (assuming you have a choice), you should define your field of operations as specifically as possible, and be clear about your ultimate aims. If you ambition is to start up a business in one area and then expand elsewhere, or even to build up a great organisation, you must be sure to choose a business that is capable of such growth. If, however, your sole ambition is to make a comfortable living and sell or close down the firm when you retire, do not choose a business which can only survive by continually growing and expanding.

preparation

Deciding when to start will need to be related to the amount of money at your disposal: there is likely to be a period during which you will be paying all the outgoings, with little or no money coming in, while your own living expenses will still have to be met.

Begin by taking stock of your resources and assets, both human and financial. Human assets include your own skills and energy, and those of any member of your family who will be working with you.

Most people starting in business lack one or more of the basic skills needed for success. It is usually cheaper in the long run to buy in a missing skill, say a clerk or book-keeper, than attempt the figure and paper work yourself unless you really know what you are doing. Not only will you take longer than a skilled person and make more mistakes, but spending the same amount of time in using your own skill (selling, for example) will make more money for the business eventually.

skills to learn

There are certain skills for which you have to pay others that are worth learning, such as typing, the first elements of accountancy, business administration. If you intend to have a partner, perhaps your own husband or wife, divide up between you who will learn what, at evening classes perhaps, through books, by correspondence course – quite apart from reading around the main subjects of your enterprise.

Get used to the idea that, however knowledgeable you may be in your own field, there is a lot to learn. And make sure that you take advantage of the various sources of help. Just now, a large number of *Start your own business* training courses are available. They may be run by the local authority, or by one of the many small firms agencies.

The Manpower Services Commission is responsible for various courses ranging from one week to sixteen weeks. The fees may be paid for and a training allowance given to people who are unemployed and have been out of full time education for at least 2 years. For details of courses in your area, ask at the local MSC office, or get in touch with ▲ Manpower Services Commission, Moorfoot, Sheffield 1S1 4PQ (telephone: 0742-753275).

getting advice

Anyone who has previously always been an employee may find that making decisions without any help is very difficult.

You may have friends who are professional people – accountant, bank manager, solicitor – willing to give you advice, perhaps initially without charging.

Do not be too proud to get advice, lots of it. Although the bank manager is employed to look after the bank's interest, which may not be the same as your interest, it can be helpful to get his opinion even if he is not providing the funds.

It may take months before you can start. You may need to find premises with all the delays that that involves (including, perhaps, planning permission and equipping them). If your business project is not based on something you are doing already, it is a good idea to make it into a spare-time pursuit, while continuing with your job and getting some experience of the work without burning your boats.

Where to go for money and advice

By and large, money will always be forthcoming for a sound project, well presented. If you cannot get money for your project, either there is some flaw in it, or you have not presented it to the best advantage. If you ask your bank manager for a loan or overdraft on the basis of a few figures on the back of an envelope, you will scarcely inspire confidence.

The obvious source of finance is the bank. Buying money is not very different from buying anything else. Banks make their profits from lending money and they want your business, provided they are sure they will not lose by it. It is best to approach your own bank in the first instance; the manager knows the state of your account, and if you are generally solvent and in control of your outgoings, this will give him some confidence in you. You may get a rapid response: some bank managers take pride in their powers of swift assessment and decision. But if you do not, rather than just waiting for an answer which may turn out to be 'no', approach two or three other commercial institutions.

where the money may come from

If you own high-street bank refuses, try the other clearing banks, any of which may provide the finance. There are also numerous merchant banks able to provide medium-term finance. If your project is closely associated with another country, an approach to one of the country's banks might bring results.

Many banks have developed special schemes for helping new businesses: they include unsecured loan schemes, and loans with capital repayment deferred. It is therefore worthwhile to investigate various banks as possible sources.

Another line of attack is provided by the Industrial and Commercial Finance Corporation (ICFC), a subsidiary of the Finance for Industry Group (FFI), jointly owned by the Bank of England and the English and Scottish clearing banks, and using funds from the private sector. ICFC specialises in lending to businesses which have been unable to raise money through bank loans in the usual way; it also offers advisory services. It may require some form of equity participation (that is, a

share in the business) depending on the type of finance requested, and the kind of business it is needed for. However, it does not generally finance start-ups, or businesses requiring less than £5,000. Contact the
▲ head office at 91 Waterloo Road, London SE1 8XP (telephone: 01-928 7822) for the address of your local area office.

If your new business is technologically innovative, you could approach Technical Development Capital (TDC), a subsidiary of ICFC, which specialises in helping small to middle-sized firms to exploit the commercial potential of technological advances.

There is a government-sponsored organisation offering similar aid, with emphasis on the exploitation of new technology: the British Technology Group (BTG) which can provide joint-venture finance for projects based on technical innovation in any field of technology. The organisation will contribute up to half the project's cost not only for technological development work but capital for plant and tooling, and working capital, and the expenses of bringing the product on to the market. If the project results in sales, the BTG will ask for a percentage levy, but if the project is not commercially successful, the finance will not have to be repaid. There are no formal minimum or maximum amounts of investment for any single project.

The British Technology Group also provides recirculating loans which are working capital loans for machinery or equipment to tide a company over the manufacturing period; once the product has been delivered and payment received, the loan has to be repaid to the BTG. But a further venture can be financed by another recirculating loan.

The BTG has a Small Companies Division which administers schemes specially intended to help the smaller firms, both technology-based and more traditional businesses.

Further information can be requested from the British Technology
▲ Group, 101 Newington Causeway, London SE1 6BU (telephone: 01-403 6666).

help depending on location

The government offers aid and financial incentives to firms starting up in those areas where it is anxious to encourage employment; development areas, and enterprise zones. The Small Firms Division of the Department of Industry, which has information centres and area counselling offices throughout the UK, will tell you where these assisted areas are. The aid offered is in the form of subsidies and grants.

If you intend to operate in an assisted area, you can apply for a regional development grant. There are two sizes of grant depending on whether the request comes for a development area or a special development area. They are 50 per cent and 22 per cent respectively of 'eligible expenditures' for new buildings, adaptation of existing buildings, new machinery and plant. But there are minimum requirements, for instance the cost of plant must be over £500 for a small firm.

Grants are available not only for manufacturing business but also for new offices and service industries setting up in, or moving to assisted areas if new jobs are thereby created.

There is a booklet with full information: *Regional Development Grants Notes for Applicants* published by the Department of Industry and ▲ available from Kingsgate House, 66-74 Victoria Street, London SW1E 6SJ.

A business that is set up in an enterprise zone may be able to take advantage of certain tax concessions and rating allowances.

The Council for Small Industries in Rural Areas (CoSIRA) offers advice and also loans to applicants who employ not more than 20 skilled people. The loans are for buildings, equipment and also working capital. The minimum loan is £250, the maximum is £50,000, but the loan is never more than 80 per cent of the cost of the particular project. Interest is payable on the loan at a slightly lower rate than what the commercial market charges.

There are some 30 local CoSIRA organisers who help with problems of the small business in rural areas, also including country towns of up to 10,000 inhabitants. Further information for England can be ▲ obtained from the headquarters of CoSIRA at 141 Castle Street, Salisbury, Wiltshire SP1 3TP (telephone: Salisbury 6255). The related bodies in Wales are the Small Business Section of the Welsh Devel- ▲ opment Agency, Treeforest Industrial Estate, Pontypridd, Mid Glamorgan, CF37 5UT (telephone: Treeforest 2666), and in Scotland, ▲ the Scottish Development Agency (Small Business Division) 102 Telford Road, Edinburgh EN4 2NP (telephone: 031-343 1911). In North-

▲ ern Ireland, it is the Local Enterprise Development Unit, Lamont House, Purdys Lane, Newtownbreda, Belfast 8 (telephone: 0232 691031).

In some of the major cities too, local authorities have created similar support agencies, designed to encourage industry back into parts of inner urban areas. These are administered by the Department of the Environment, through the local authorities making grants or loans to help buy land or renovate buildings, or to help pay the rent for existing industrial or commercial premises. Some of these loans are interest free.

presenting your case

Government help, or local government help, is by no means automatically available even where such stipulations as the creation of fresh employment are met. One prerequisite in all cases is that the proposed business must show itself likely to be viable.

In some cases it is stipulated that the presentation of a proposal must conform to a standard form, which may include an independent accountant's report. Each organisation has its own set of rules, so the proposal should be written to satisfy these rules. The information that the funding organisations need, and the way it is presented, should be very carefully prepared: it is almost a professional task. In any event, it is probably worth involving an accountant at this stage, if only to help you present a cash flow forecast.

CoSIRA offers help in drawing up funding propositions for presentation to the ICFC or to the bank.

The bank itself may help you with a cash flow forecast: all the major banks run some form of business advisory service, free to customers, but this help is mainly intended for established businesses. However, many of the banks publish booklets intended for the person who wants to start a business.

new enterprise help

Perhaps the best place to go to is one of the organisations whose primary aim is helping the small or new entrepreneur. Amongst these

is the Small Firms Service (SFS) of the Department of Industry (Small
▲ Firms Division), Ashdown House, 123 Victoria Street, London SW1
6RB, freefone 244) whose many (free) publications include *Setting up
a new business*. Local Small Firms Centres arrange one-to-one meetings
for discussing problems with experienced businessmen. The initial
meeting is free.

In London, the activities of LEntA, the London Enterprise Agency,
include a training programme with one-day conferences giving an
introduction to the basic requirements for starting and running a
business, or an advanced course of four linked weekends. There is also
a counselling service dealing with finance and help in presenting a case
to providers of finance.

▲ An organisation called Business in the Community, 91 Waterloo Road,
London SE1 8XP (telephone: 01-928 6423) has published a 24 page
directory of enterprise agencies, in alphabetical order of towns by
location. They may be sponsored by local industry (for instance the
Shropshire Enterprise Trust in Telford) or by the local authority (for
instance Coventry City Council's Business Advice Centre) or a mixture
of both (the Fens Business Enterprise Trust in Wisbech).

Also, in an appendix to *Information and the Small Manufacturing Firm*
(Report by Capital Planning Information Ltd for the British Library),
available through public libraries, there is an alphabetical list of public
and private enterprises and action resource centres, with their addresses
(from Aid to Bristol to Wolverhampton Enterprise Limited).

But whoever helps you present your case, make sure that you, yourself,
understand the calculations, because it is you who will have to explain
and justify them to the bank manager or other potential lender, and
it will be your responsibility to produce the results to match them.
Your forecast must demonstrate, not only that you have coherent and
realistic plans for the future, but also that you will be monitoring your
progress against them, week by week, month by month, and are
unlikely to be overwhelmed by unforeseen disasters.

what the bank manager wants to know

Make an appointment and say why you want to see the bank manager. If you are a customer of his, he will want to look up your banking record before you see him, to assure himself that you can handle your money responsibly. A past overdraft will not be held against you, provided it was by arrangement, not inadvertence. If you are not a customer, he will ask for references from your own bank.

He will want to know what kind of business you want to set up; what kind and size of market you expect to trade in; the likely extent of the competition; how you propose to go about marketing your product.

He will ask why you consider yourself particularly qualified for this business; whether you have experience of it, for how long and with what success; and whether you have sought expert advice. He will want to know exactly what resources you have, which may include redundancy money, savings, stocks and shares and other securities and investments, valuables convertible into cash; and the value of your house and car. He will want to know where the rest of the financing of your enterprise will come from (including other loans, perhaps a loan from a member of the family, at low interest). He will want to know how much you want to borrow, for how long and how you propose to pay it back. He is likely to want to see a budget and a cash flow forecast for at least 12 months which will demonstrate that the loan can be repaid.

The bank manager will, perhaps surprisingly, want to be sure that you are not asking for too little money. Many beginner businessmen are too modest in their requirements: they do not take account of all the overheads to be paid for, and forget to make provision for slack times in the trade, or unforeseen contingencies, such as a dock strike affecting export business. So, if in doubt, ask for more rather than less.

offering security

The question of what security you can offer is bound to arise. A bank may lend without it, but only on an exceptionally sound proposition, and not always then.

A life insurance policy is unlikely to bring in much if you surrender it to provide capital for your business, but it may be acceptable as security for a bank loan. If you own a house or other real estate, you can use it as security for a loan or overdraft, provided that it is freehold, or on a long lease (over 20 years left, say) but the bank's estimate of its value will certainly be a good deal lower than yours, even after you deduct the amount owing on a first mortgage.

An alternative to consider would be selling your house and moving to a cheaper one or a rented one to provide more start-up capital. If you intend to buy or rent a factory from a local authority, especially in a development area, this may secure you a high place on the housing list.

You may feel that to part with the roof over the family's head is too rash, but the people you will be asking for a loan will expect you to carry a portion of the risk. It is important to know that most financial organisations will expect your own stake in the business to equal theirs.

There is a loan guarantee scheme which helps small businesses to raise loans from commercial sources where a loan would not have been granted without such guarantee. The Department of Industry may guarantee up to four-fifths of the loan but the applicant must generally be willing to pledge all his assets as security for the guaranteed loan.

Full information about this scheme can be obtained from the Loan ▲ Guarantee Unit of the Department of Industry, Abell House, John Islip Street, London SW1P 4LN (telephone: 01-211 5970).

It is very easy, in the desperation of trying to raise capital for a project about which you are very enthusiastic, to give too much security to your source of finance, leaving nothing for future borrowing.

About finance before you start

Whatever your project, you should have a picture in your mind of what stage you intend to have reached in one or two years' time, even if you cannot make anything but a very approximate forecast about this. What matters is having a forward plan, against which you will be able to monitor your progress. If things go according to plan, it will give your confidence a boost. And if things are not going as planned, you will be able right away to take whatever action is necessary.

There are some essential basic concepts you must understand, such as overheads, materials and labour costs, unit costs, start-up capital, working capital, short-term and medium-term finance, cash flow, profit and loss account.

The cost of producing anything is made up of a number of elements; how many are involved depends on whether it is a product or a service. Reduced to their simplest terms, they are as follows:

Cost of materials from which products are made: the cost of materials in one year, divided by the number of units of the product manufactured in that year, gives the materials cost per unit.

For a retailer or wholesaler, his materials are his stock of goods. An agent or consultant has no materials costs.

Direct labour costs: in a manufacturing business, the before-tax wages paid to the people who actually make the product (not the wages of ancillary workers such as sales and office staff).

To find the labour cost per unit, divide the total annual labour costs by the number of product units.

overheads

All business costs that do not come under materials or labour are classified as overheads. Generally speaking, these are the standing costs of the business which must be paid whether or not you succeed in making and selling anything.

In the annual accounts, overheads are classified under the following headings:

Salaries and wages	before-tax remuneration paid to office and sales staff, also directors' salaries and any other money they draw out of the business
Rent and rates	
Heating, lighting and other services	gas, electricity, oil, propane gas, water and sewerage, etc
Advertising/marketing	(excluding the cost of any special launch)
Printing, postage and stationery, telephone, telex, etc	all office supplies and expenses
Motor and travel expenses	tax, insurance, servicing and repairs, petrol; expenses of travel by other means
Leasing and/or hire charges	
Insurances	
Professional fees	accountant, solicitor, patent agent
Depreciation	including motor vehicles
Interest on loans and overdraft	rough estimate
Sundry expenses	

Every single one of the overhead costs must be allowed for when you are working out what to charge for a unit of your product or an hour of your time. If you underestimate your overheads, you may find that far from making a profit, you are actually working at a loss.

costing your products

Estimate, pessimistically, how many units of your product you will make and sell in your first year of full production, given your present resources. Work out the total overheads cost for this period. By dividing the second figure by the first, you get the overheads cost per unit. Thus, if the estimated production is 10,000 units and total overheads are £20,000, you must add £2 to the materials and labour cost of each unit, to break even.

But, of course, you want to do better than just cover your costs, so you add to your break-even figure an amount which will be your profit.

costing in a service industry

The principle is similar, except that instead of charging per unit of product, you will charge per hour of the time spent by you or a member of your staff in actually doing a job. Overheads usually represent the chief element of costs of the business. If you are, for instance, a washing-machine engineer, or a plumber, your charge for an hour of your time should include travelling time and expenses, the cost of your tools and equipment, and the wages of the person who answers your telephone and makes out your invoices: all these are overheads. And the chief element in the overheads will be salaries or wages which have to be paid (including to yourself) whether or not anyone is actually out on a job.

If your total overheads costs come to £8,000 for an estimated total of 1,000 job-hours per year, your break-even price per hour will be £8. If you have to replace the machine's drum or motor you will have to charge the customer separately for materials.

what is start-up capital?

This is the 'once-for-all' expenditure needed to start a new business, the cash you must lay out before you have manufactured a single item, or dealth with a single client. Unless you start off in your garage with a secondhand typewriter, you will have to pay for some, though not necessarily all, of the following:

- premises: buying or rebuilding, conversion or even building from scratch

- plant and equipment, tools
- goodwill, if taking over an existing business
- office equipment and furniture
- installation of electricity, gas, telephone and any other services
- initial administrative costs: legal and other professional fees
- stationery: the paper, envelopes, postcards, invoices etc printed with the firm's name
- publicity: cost of the initial launch.

You should assess this expenditure as accurately as possible and consider ways of reducing it if necessary (for instance, by delaying any pieces of plant not immediately needed, or by leasing or hiring plant instead of buying).

When you begin to work out how much money you are going to need for your project, you must be sure to include not only the start-up capital (the money needed to get your business going) but also the working capital (the money you need to keep on going in the interval between your outgoings and your receipts).

what is working capital?

In a manufacturing industry, once production starts, some weeks or even months must pass before the products are finished, sold, despatched and paid for. In the meantime, you must keep paying for materials, labour and overheads: the cost of all of these represents your working capital.

If you need to keep large stocks of raw materials or finished products or have a number of people on the payroll, materials costs and labour costs will be tied up without, for the time being, any returns. Your working capital will therefore need to be so much the greater. If your suppliers give you 30 days' credit, and your customers pay cash in 7 days (in return for a small discount, perhaps), your working capital requirement will be reduced. At the same time, you will speed up your cash flow, that is, the rate at which money passes out of and into your business. Working capital and cash flow are closely related: the more money you have lying stagnant – in materials, stock, or in customers' unpaid invoices – the more working capital you will need.

In the retail and distributive trades (that is, a shop), where the goods held in stock represent the materials costs, the amount of working capital needed and the rate of cash flow depend on the amount of unsold stock, not so much on unpaid invoices because the retail trade has the advantage that customers generally pay straightway. A service industry, without stocks of materials or direct labour costs, needs comparatively little working capital: enough to pay overhead costs till the money starts coming in.

short-term finance

As the name suggests, it is money required for short periods of time. It may be needed for start-up capital or for temporary increases in working capital.

If you are setting up a service business or an agency, or plan to be a middleman rather than a manufacturer, you may need little in the way of plant and labour, and consequently a comparatively small start-up capital. But you may still need short-term money, to cover the interval between your outgoings and your receipts.

Such short-term finance can be in the form of a loan for a stated amount, generally with a fixed interest rate and repayment date, or an overdraft. An overdraft usually has a top limit beyond which you cannot borrow, and interest is calculated on a daily basis, and varies according to the prevailing base rate. An overdraft is usually one of the cheapest forms of borrowing even though there may be a setting-up charge. Its great disadvantage is that it is repayable on demand – though banks seldom do call it in over the short term.

medium-term finance

This is money repayable in 3 to 7 years, and is usually needed as start-up capital to pay for plant and equipment, but it may be working capital. In the past, it was possible to borrow at a fixed rate of interest, but now, with frequent fluctuations in the base rate, a variable rate is more common. The fixed-rate loan, if you can get it, is something of a gamble – you stand to lose if interest rates fall – but it does give the advantage of stability: you know exactly how much you will have to pay for your loan, which is a help in making estimates. It is generally possible to repay a loan before it is due and you must be able to pay off the full amount by the stated date.

cash flow forecasting

At any given time, there will be a difference between your outgoings and your receipts, which has to be covered from funds available in reserve, or by bank overdraft or other forms of credit.

Cash flow forecasting is calculating what this difference will be, based on month by month predictions (or, rather, educated guesses) about the times when you will be paying out and when you will be collecting money, over a period of, say, six months or a year.

The outgoings, which are largely predictable, include wages (the payment of which can never be postponed), and materials (remember that some suppliers insist on cash on delivery), VAT (which has to be paid quarterly and is refunded to you quarterly, so it is also a reliable source of receipts), overheads (which for the calculations have to be averaged out).

averaging out overheads

Your overheads will include major bills payable at different intervals: rent once a year, rates probably twice yearly, electricity, gas and telephone once a quarter. All these will be entered in the books as they are paid, making for an irregular pattern in your accounting, with several bills in some months, and none in others. So, for the purpose of making monthly comparisons or cash flow predictions, total up all your overheads for one year, and include one-twelfth of the total in each month's calculations.

receipts

The calculation of receipts is less predictable. The level of sales is likely to fluctuate from month to month. Some customers pay cash in 7 days, usually expecting to be rewarded by a cash discount (negotiated in advance), others pay in 30 or 60 days (also by previous arrangement). There are bad customers and bad debts, so that part of your money may be outstanding for a long time – or forever: you should allow an estimated sum for this in each month's receipts calculations.

It is because outgoings are more predictable than receipts that cash flow forecasting is so essential, right from the start: you may have to provide funds for wages, materials and overheads for some months during which there is little or nothing coming in.

The cash flow forecast indicates the actual movement of money, not promises to pay: it is concerned strictly with what comes in and goes out, and the time of each transaction. If you intend to raise capital by borrowing from a bank, the manager will want to examine your cash flow forecast in order to assess your ability to control your financial resources. And your bank manager will also want to see a profit and loss forecast.

how to set up a profit and loss forecast

Start by choosing a target: the amount of turnover you think you can achieve in one year's time. Use as the break-even figure the minimum amount you need for your business and personal expenses, and decide how soon you have to reach that point.

Your turnover will need to increase steadily month by month in order to reach the target figure on time. Work out a set of projected monthly turnover figures, and arrange them on a 12-month table.

A practical example, using manufactured products to set out the various problems is that of Bill, a newly-started small scale manufacturer (but exactly the same method would be used for any other kind of business).

Bill, who is ambitious and confident of his market, plans to achieve a turnover of £50,000 a month by the end of the first year, so he plans his first year's turnover as in line (1) in table A (*on page 26*).

PROJECTED PROFIT AND LOSS ACCOUNT. (figures in £'s 000)

month	1	2	3	4	5	6	7	8	9	10	11	12	TOTAL	% OF SALES.
sales receipts less VAT. ①	1	3	6	10	15	20	25	30	35	40	45	50	280	100
less materials purchased. ②	0·5	1·5	3	5	7·5	10	12·5	15	17·5	20	22·5	25	140	50
less direct labour. ③	0·3	0·9	1·8	3	4·5	6	7·5	9	10·5	12	13·5	15	84	30
gross profit. ④	0·2	0·6	1·2	2	3	4	5	6	7	8	9	10	56	20
overheads. ⑤	4	4	4	4	4	4	4	4	4	4	4	4	48	17
net profit. ⑥	(3·8)	(3·4)	(2·8)	(2·0)	(1·0)	—	1	2	3	4	5	6	8	3

Bill's TABLE A (figures in brackets are deficit), figures are in £000.

Bill enters in line (2) his cost of materials, which he estimates as a percentage (namely 50 per cent) of sales. He plans to use part-time labour in the first instance, building up to full-time employees as and when they can be justified. His labour figures, again a rough estimate, are expressed in line (3) as a percentage of sales (namely 30 per cent).

By subtracting the labour and materials costs from the receipts, Bill finds his monthly gross profit, in line (4).

In the case of a single-handed owner in a small service industry – say, a plumber – there would be no labour and materials costs, all expenses being charged as overheads, and the sales figures would also be the gross profit figures. In a retail or wholesale business, the materials would be the purchases of stock.

Bill knows that his overheads will vary from month to month: he therefore averages them over 12 months, in line (5). The resulting set of figures, in line (6), is his monthly net profit, which shows him when he can expect to start making money. It will take him six months to break even, and he will begin to make a satisfactory profit after his turnover has topped £30,000.

the next step

Estimating profits is, however, only half of the story. The second, and more important half, is being in control of the cash flow. However, much profit you expect to be making by the end of the first year, your estimates will be in vain if in the meantime you cannot meet your suppliers' invoices, or your overhead expenses – not to mention the living expenses of you and your family.

cash flow forecast

Table B shows how Bill works out his cash flow forecast.

He reckons that he needs about £15,000 to buy plant, machinery and office furnishing. He plans to sell his present car (and lease a small van). This, with his redundancy money, means that he has some £7,000 in the bank. He has persuaded his father-in-law to let him have a further £5,000 if it is required, as a stand-by interest-free loan, to be repaid from profits.

He bases his calculations on the same 12-month scheme as his profit and loss forecast, entering his £7,000 as his bank balance in line (1) in the first month.

He estimates his monthly payments to suppliers in line (2): they are the materials costs from his first forecast, but now including VAT at 15 per cent, and must be paid in cash, as Bill has not yet become credit-worthy.

For line (3) Bill reckons that he can spread his capital payments (for plant and equipment) over the six months during which he will be building up his turnover.

Wages and salaries (including National Insurance contributions) in line (4) must be paid promptly, and VAT at 15 per cent in line (5) must be paid on sales and falls due quarterly from the end of the third month. The overheads in line (6) which include Bill's living expenses are averaged out, as before.

Bill finds each month's borrowing requirement in line (7) by adding up his outgoings – lines (2) to (6) inclusive – and subtracting them from that month's opening balance in line (1), (or, where the balance is negative, adding them as an increase of indebtedness to that month's overdraft).

It is obvious to Bill that he is going to require his father-in-law's money. So that £5,000 goes in, in line (8).

He will not start getting his receipts from sales, in line (9), until the second month. From the end of the third month he will be getting quarterly VAT refunds, in line (10). His last set of figures in line (11), the closing bank balance/deficit, shows Bill's final borrowing requirement.

PROJECTED CASH FLOW. (figures in £'s 000)

month	1	2	3	4	5	6	7	8	9	10	11	12
① Opening bank balance (overdraft)	7	5·13	(6·35)	(13·16)	(19·58)	(27·21)	(34·46)	(37·94)	(41·44)	(41·54)	(47·06)	(44·44)
② PAYMENTS to suppliers.	0·57	1·73	3·45	5·75	8·63	11·5	14·38	17·25	20·1	23·0	25·88	28·75
③ Capital Payments.	2	5	2	1	2	3						
④ Wages and Salaries. (inc. N.I.)	0·3	0·9	1·6	3	4·5	6	7·5	9	10·5	12	13·5	15·0
⑤ VAT payments.				1·5			6·75			13·5		
⑥ Overheads.	4	4	4	4	4	4	4	4	4	4	4	4
⑦ Maximum Borrowing Requirement.	0·13	(6·60)	(1·60)	(28·40)	(38·71)	(51·71)	(67·09)	(70·19)	(76·04)	(94·04)	(90·44)	(92·19)
⑧ RECEIPTS Loans/Capital introduced.	5											
⑨ Receipts from sales.	—	1·15	3·45	6·90	11·50	17·25	23·00	28·75	34·50	40·25	46·00	51·75
⑩ VAT refunds.				1·92			4·15			6·73		
⑪ Closing bank balance (projected borrowing)	5·13	(6·35)	(13·16)	(19·58)	(27·21)	(34·46)	(37·94)	(41·44)	(41·54)	(47·06)	(44·44)	(40·64)

Bill's TABLE B (figures in brackets are deficit), figures are in £000.

He now looks at his cash flow situation month by month. After the first month's outgoings, his capital has dwindled to a mere £130. After adding to his credit balance the £5,000 loan, he carries forward to month 2 an opening balance of £5,130.

By the end of month 2, Bill's credit balance has turned into an overdraft of £5,350, even with the receipts from the first month's sales; this, too, is carried forward. His borrowing requirement increases steadily, and by the end of the year his overdraft is over £40,000.

Bill may well be surprised, when comparing his two forecasts, the profit and loss and the cash flow, to find that his happy expectation of breaking even at a turnover of £20,000 within six months has turned into a funding requirement of about £35,000 over and above his original investment, even though he has assumed that his turnover will remain stable at £50,000 a month.

In order to avoid a cash flow crisis – running out of funds – Bill looks at ways of reducing his outgoings. He fixes on a less ambitious turnover target of £40,000, and aims for a faster growth in sales so that he will break even in month 5. By leasing instead of buying some of his plant, he reduces his capital repayments, but incurs leasing charges as shown in line (6). He thus almost halves his final borrowing requirement, and his amended profit and loss and cash flow forecasts (tables C and D) make a more convincing presentation for the bank manager's eye. They have to be adjusted to allow for the interest, at whatever is the current rate, on the money to be borrowed.

not borrowing but leasing

Leasing is a form of getting medium-term finance without the need to borrow money. The plant, equipment and vehicles you need are bought by a finance company and then leased to you for an agreed rent. At the end of the contract, the equipment may be offered to you for sale at a low price, or you may be able to continue leasing it at a reduced rental.

If you lease most of your plant and other equipment, you will be able to get tax relief on some of the cost.

AMENDED PROJECTED PROFIT AND LOSS ACCOUNT. (figures in £'s 000)

month	1	2	3	4	5	6	7	8	9	10	11	12	TOTAL	% OF SALES
sales receipts less VAT. ①	3	6	10	15	20	25	30	35	35	40	40	40	299	100
less materials purchased. ②	1·5	3	5	7·5	10	12·5	15	17·5	17·5	20	20	20	149·4	50
less direct labour. ③	0·9	1·8	3·0	4·5	6·0	7·5	9·0	10·5	10·5	12	12	12	89·7	30
gross profit. ④	0·6	1·2	2·0	3·0	4·0	5·0	6·0	7·0	7·0	8·0	8·0	8·0	59·8	20
overheads. ⑤	4	4	5	4	4	5	4	4	5	4	4	5	52·0	17·3
net profit ⑥	(3·4)	(2·8)	(3·0)	(1·0)	—	—	2	3	2	4	4	3	7·8	2·7

Bill's TABLE C

AMENDED PROJECTED CASH FLOW.

(figures in £'s 000)

month	1	2	3	4	5	6	7	8	9	10	11	12
① Opening bank balance/(overdraft)	7	3.37	(3.43)	(12.28)	(19.69)	(23.68)	(27.56)	(33.43)	(33.53)	(28.88)	(36.14)	(28.14)
② PAYMENTS to suppliers.	1.73	3.45	5.75	8.63	11.5	14.38	17.25	20.10	20.10	23.00	23.00	23.00
③ Capital Payments.	2	1	2	1								
④ Wages and Salaries (inc. N.I.)	0.9	1.8	3.0	4.5	6.0	7.5	9.0	10.5	10.5	12.0	12.0	12.0
⑤ VAT payments.				2.85			9.0			15.00		
⑥ Overheads.	4	4	5	4	4	5	4	4	5	4	4	5
⑦ Maximum Borrowing Requirement.	(1.63)	(6.88)	(19.18)	(33.28)	(41.18)	(50.56)	(66.81)	(68.03)	(69.13)	(82.88)	(74.14)	(68.14)
⑧ RECEIPTS Loans/Capital introduced.	5											
⑨ Receipts from sales.	—	3.45	6.90	11.5	17.25	23.00	28.75	34.50	40.25	40.25	46.06	46.00
⑩ VAT refunds.	—			2.08			4.63			7.49		
⑪ Closing bank balance/(projected bottoming).	3.57	(3.43)	(12.28)	(19.68)	(23.68)	(27.56)	(33.43)	(33.53)	(28.58)	(35.14)	(28.14)	(22.14)

Bill's TABLE D

The main advantage of leasing is that your working capital is not tied up in rapidly depreciating machinery and you can reduce your borrowing needs.

The first approach to the lessor has to come from you, the potential lessee. If you are new to the company, a bank reference (but usually no security) is required. You have to specify exactly what equipment you want and, if the deal is approved, the lessor buys it new from the manufacturer and leases it to you on the agreed terms.

Some equipment is leased for short periods, generally office or computer equipment, and can later be exchanged for more up-to-date models. The contract may provide that the leasing company should be responsible for maintaining the equipment.

▲ The address of the Equipment Leasing Association is 18 Upper Grosvenor Street, London, W1 (telephone: 01-491 2783). You can ask for a booklet *Equipment Leasing* and a list of leasing companies to be sent to you, most of which are London-based but operate in any part of the country.

Hire-purchase is another way of obtaining plant and equipment without capital outlay. Just as in domestic purchases, you pay a deposit and then regular fixed instalments, and at the end of the contract the goods become your property. The instalment payments are generally higher than interest on a bank loan, but you may not wish to, or be able to, increase your bank loan.

looking at the figures

Bill's case has several vital lessons for the new entrepreneur. First of all, you will certainly be surprised when you discover just how much money you are going to need as working capital. It is easy to underestimate one's requirements. Many companies which are expanding make that mistake: they run out of money because they expand too rapidly. This is called overtrading.

Secondly, an estimated profit margin may appear ample, yet, unless the volume of sales is great beyond all reasonable expectation, the total profits may fail to cover outgoings.

Nearly every first attempt at a profit and loss forecast is too ambitious. That is why a cash flow forecast is needed: to warn the small businessman when his resources are not equal to his ambitions.

It is easy to recast figures at the planning stage in order to deploy one's resources to best advantage, and arrive at a satisfactory and realistic forecast which can confidently be put before a bank or other financial organisation. However, it is terribly easy, when you have produced a forecast you do not like, to adjust the assumptions and figures – in that order – so that it all looks workable. You must look at original assumptions and new ones and see if you are not introducing too much wishful thinking.

why you will need an accountant

If you already know something about business accounting and revel in figures, you may think that you can do without an accountant.

Bear in mind, however, that however nimble with numbers you may be, you are unlikely to have an accountant's grasp of the innumerable regulations relating to taxation or the relevant aspects of company and revenue law, nor his experience in dealing with the Board of Inland Revenue, nor his all-round familiarity with different aspects of business. Here are some of the problems in which an accountant can help you:

- to decide whether to set up as a sole trader, partnership or a limited company
- to find ways of raising capital
- to set up cash flow forecasts and profit and loss forecasts
- to decide whether to register for VAT if you do not have to
- to choose a starting date, and more important still, a trading-year end date
- to keep day-to-day records, account books and ledgers
- to claim all possible allowances and reliefs against tax, and to negotiate with the tax inspector
- to cope with pensions, annuities and insurance.

How are you going to trade?

You will have to decide whether to trade as a sole trader, in a partnership, or as a limited company. There is the possibility, in most cases, of changing to another legal entity later, as your business develops.

sole trader

Being a sole trader does not mean that you have to work alone but that you are totally and solely responsible for the business: you take all the profits, but you are also personally liable for all the debts incurred to the full extent of your means. Should you not have the money to pay your business debts, your personal possessions could be taken in settlement. This includes even your clothes and the tools of your trade, not to speak of your house and home.

Many small businesses start as sole traders and later become limited companies, for tax reasons.

partnership

A business partnership is an association of two or more people (up to 20) trading together as one firm and sharing the profits. A single tax assessment is made on the profits of a partnership, so that what is shared out represents post-tax profits. And if one partner should abscond, the others have to pay all the outstanding tax, including what would have been the absconder's share.

It is wise, in a partnership, to have a simple agreement, drawn up by a solicitor, and setting out each partner's share of the profits, and how each partner's share is to be valued if he wants to withdraw from the partnership, or a new partner comes in and, if one of the partners dies, what should happen to his share. In cases of losses, all the partners can be held liable for the whole of the firm's debts, to the full extent of their personal means, just as though they were a sole trader.

The agreement should state for how long the partnership is to run or under what conditions it can be terminated. Partnerships that go sour can be messy and upsetting, so it is wise to lay down guide lines of who does what and what should happen in the case of a dispute. All the partners may work in the firm, or there may be a 'sleeping partner' who just puts in money. A partnership agreement can include any clauses specific to the particular set of circumstances.

Sole traders and partnerships may trade under their own name or names, or else under other name or title. However, if the name that you have chosen to trade under is not your own surname(s), you must indicate the name(s) of the owner(s) on all stationery, and display them in your shop or office or place or work.

limited company

A limited company is a legal entity, just as though it were a person, and must be conducted according to rules laid down by company law. They include the maintenance of accounts, an annual audit, and the disclosure of the company's activities to the general public.

The shareholders, of whom there must be at least two, are the owners of the company, but are liable for its debts only to the extent of the face value of their shares. However, a director's liability can be extended by personal guarantees that he may have given to a bank or other financial institution as security for a business loan.

Limited companies may be public or private. If public ('P.L.C.'), the shares are available to the general public and are generally quoted on the Stock Exchange.

Private companies – the majority – are our chief concern here; they do not offer shares to the public, and style themselves 'Limited' or 'Ltd'.

formalities

A limited company must be registered by the Registrar of Companies, ▲ Companies House, Crown Way, Maindy, Cardiff, CF4 3UZ (telephone: 0222 388588), for Scotland, Companies Registration Office, ▲ 102 George Street, Edinburgh, EH2 3DJ (telephone: 031-2555774).

Registration entails submitting a memorandum of association which must include details of the name of the company, its registered address, the objects of the company, statement of the limited liability of its members, the amount of share capital and how it is divided into shares. It must be properly signed and witnessed.

The Registrar of Companies will send, on request, a pamphlet *Notes for the Guidance on Incorporation of New Companies (C 56)*.

It is important to have professional help in registering a company. Some lawyers and accountants specialise in this.

Also, there are company registration agents, through whom you can 'buy' a company off the shelf. The agent has registered the company with stand-in directors, shareholders and secretary, but the company is not operating. When you buy the company, your names are substituted for those of the stand-ins.

If you buy a ready-made company, you will not be trading under your own name and must therefore comply with the disclosure rules which demand that the names of owners and the registered address are displayed in a number of places including all the business stationery. (*Notes for Guidance on control of business name* can be obtained from
▲ the Department of Trade Guidance Note Section, 55 City Road, London EC1 Y1B or from Companies House.)

co-operative

If your project is likely to employ people right from the beginning, you might find it advantageous to start a co-operative; there are specialised agencies which give help with this.

A co-operative is a business enterprise which is jointly owned by its members; these are, as a rule, the people who work in it, but people associated with the enterprise in other ways, such as suppliers, or friends and relations may, in some cases, also become members.

A co-operative may be a co-ownership, with the workers owning shares in the equity of the business in proportion to their investment in it; or it may be a common ownership, with the assets being collectively owned.

A co-operative may be registered under the Industrial and Provident Societies Acts, with members having limited liability; it may be a partnership; or it may be incorporated as a limited company. A registered co-operative must always have at least seven members, not all of whom need be workers in the co-operative.

What is of the essence of a co-operative is that it is run for the benefit of its members and has a democratic constitution: each member has one vote, and thus an equal share in controlling the whole enterprise, irrespective of the size of his investment in it. This does not mean that every single decision is put to the vote: the day-to-day running of the business is usually entrusted to a management, which is accountable to the members for its decisions, and consults them on all major ones. Only a few of the 650 registered co-operatives have a permanent manager; most co-operatives operate by sharing the function of management on a rotation basis.

A co-operative must, of course, be commercially viable if it is to survive and compete with other enterprises, and must be conducted on proper business lines. However, once profits are generated, the surplus is generally distributed democratically amongst members. And though a co-operative may not need to produce a dividend, it must still be able to meet its interest payments and capital repayments on loans.

The principle of co-operation may help to keep the enterprise afloat where ordinary companies would founder. For instance, during difficult trading times members may agree to accept lower pay, or lower interest, for the good of the whole organisation.

Co-operatives may start in different ways:

take-over by workers

Sometimes, when a company is about to go into liquidation, the workers combine to keep it going by their united efforts. Such co-operatives often receive much publicity, but rescuing a failing or failed company by turning it into a co-operative is often unsuccessful unless the enterprise is scaled down.

partial buy-out

A group of workers purchases some of the assets of a company in liquidation, together with any outstanding orders, and maintains supplies of goods to customers. Many co-operatives founded in this way have been very successful.

new start

Individual entrepreneurs combine to plan and set up a co-operative, to manufacture some product or supply some service, generally in a traditional business enterprise such as printing, or building. Sometimes the nucleus of such an enterprise might be a sharing of facilities by small businesses, which may then evolve in the direction of a joint programme for marketing.

getting help

It is not easy for an individual without such previous connections to start a co-operative, but several organisations have been established to help co-operatives, and they might be able to put an aspiring co-operator in touch with others.

Among the places to go for help or information are:
▲ *Co-operative Development Agency* (CDA), 20 Albert Embankment,

London SE1 7TJ (telephone: 01-211 4633), set up by parliament to promote co-operatives. It cannot provide funds, but will give advice on setting up a co-operative; scrutinise and assess the suitability of a project; give advice on raising finance. The CDA can, on request, supply a full list of the 60 or so local co-operative development agencies which have been set up over the past few years, and of some other relevant organisations.

▲ *Industrial Common Ownership Movement* (ICOM), 7 The Corn Exchange, Leeds LS1 7BP (telephone: 0532-961737) promotes and advises co-operatives on all aspects of common ownership; produces model rules, gives legal, financial and management advice to people or enterprises who want to convert to common ownership without any outside shareholding.

▲ *Industrial Common Ownership Finance Limited* (ICOF), 1 St Giles Street, Northampton, NN1 1AA (telephone: 0604 87563) administers a revolving loan fund (in which money repaid by successful co-operatives is lent out to new and developing ones) to bona fide common ownership/co-operative enterprises. Bona fide, in this context, means being registered with ICOM.

ICOF also works directly with local authorities, either through advice and consultancy, or by administering loan funds to common ownership enterprises within the particular local authority area.

The Registrar of Friendly Societies gives information and advice about rules and registration, and issues certificates under the Industrial Common Ownership Act 1976. The addresses for different parts of ▲ the UK are 17 North Audley Street, London W1Y 2AP (telephone: ▲ 01-629 7001), for Scotland, 19 Heriot Row, Edinburgh EH3 6HD ▲ (telephone: 031-564371); and for Northern Ireland, 43/47 Chichester Street, Belfast BE1 4RJ (telephone: 0232-34121).

Beechwood College is a nationwide training and education centre for co-operative and community enterprises, which runs short and long courses and provides a research and consultancy service to local authorities and other bodies. The address is Beechwood College, Elmete ▲ Lane, Roundhay, Leeds LS8 2LQ (telephone: 0532 720205).

franchises

The principle involved in franchising is basically this: a company which is successful in manufacturing a product or providing some service decides to extend its activities in other localities. But instead of setting up its own company-owned branches, it becomes a *franchisor*, selling its experience and established reputation to individuals, the *franchisees*.

The franchisee contracts to make and sell the product, or to provide the service, under the franchisor's name and on lines laid down by the franchisor.

Well-known franchises include fast-food caterers such as Wimpy and Kentucky Fried Chicken, and service businesses such as Prontaprint and the drain cleaning Dyno-Rod. The franchisee buys himself in by paying a fixed sum, the size of which depends on the nature and extent of the business. It might be more than a million pounds for a hotel franchise, or around £7,000 for a vehicle rust-proofing service. In return, he is trained to perform the work involved and to run the business. The franchisor may help him to find premises, and will sell him the necessary equipment and materials, for which he will have to find his own financing.

Once established, the franchisee pays the franchisor a continuing royalty for the use of his name, and for back-up services such as publicity and advertising and product development. The royalty may be a percentage of the turnover, or may be collected as a mark-up on the price of the franchisor's supplies.

Buying a franchise may not be the cheapest way of starting one's own business, but the support provided by the franchisor may make it the easiest way of setting up.

The cost of setting up of a franchise is similar to, or can be more than, the cost of setting up a totally independent small business. But the franchisee buys a commercial advantage through the franchisor's expertise in a specific field and so can avoid many of the pitfalls which often trap the independent small man.

An advantage of a franchise is that the franchisee is granted exclusive rights to a particular area – as far as his franchising company is concerned (but nothing can be done to stop other companies in a similar line of business moving into the territory and competing).

It is best to deal with a franchisor who is a member of the British
▲ Franchise Association, 15 The Poynings, Iver, Bucks SL0 9DS (telephone: 0753-653546). A list of franchisors will be sent on request.

but beware . . .

Cowboy franchisors also exist. They charge a relatively high buy-in fee but offer little or no training or equipment. Or the sum involved may be low – about £5000, say, which is modest by ethical franchising standards – but when you look into what you would be getting for this, you might realise that there is very little tangible return.

The most tell-tale indicator that should serve as a warning to you is that the royalty payment is fixed, regardless of whether the business does well or badly.

So before committing yourself, visit one or more existing outlets of the franchisor and talk to the franchisee. Ask, amongst other things, whether the promised advertising and promotional support is being given, locally or nationally. Also try to find out how long the franchisor has been in operation and how many outlets he currently has.

Whoever your potential franchisor may be, let an independent accountant and/or solicitor scrutinise the financial data supplied by the franchisor and advise you on the proposed contract, including the provisions for termination of the contract.

Marketing and selling

Marketing and selling your product or service is not just an incidental appendix to producing it: it is the lifeblood of the business.

The two terms are not interchangeable. Marketing covers everything from research, product planning and development to promotion and, of course, selling. Selling is the process of negotiating and carrying out that transaction.

Emerson was mistaken: the world will not beat a path to your house to clamour for your better mousetrap. However efficient it may be, if you do not go to town and seek out people with mice, it will be left on your hands.

In fact, before you started to design it, you should have checked on the mouse population, and the cat population too; it never does to ignore one's competitors.

What is more, when you have found your customers, and are busy with orders, you must plan for future sales. Selling is a continuous process: you should always be looking ahead and planning your marketing strategy for the coming months and years.

The time to start planning for sales is when your product or service is still on the drawing-board. At this point, nothing is lost if you discover that your idea, however good of its kind, will not command a large enough market to make a profit. Perhaps it will be so expensive to produce that its price will be prohibitive; or, perhaps, there are not enough people who long for, say, reproduction antique musical boxes. You still have a chance to rethink it and eliminate expensive labour-intensive processes, for example; or modify it to give it more popular appeal; or scrap it altogether in favour of something else.

Begin by asking yourself some questions:

- What exactly have I got to offer my customers?
- Who are likely to be my customers, and where shall I find them?
- Who are my competitors, and in what way is my product an improvement on theirs or a better alternative (mousetrap v. poison)?
- What is the best way of making my product or service known to the customer?
- When do I start planning for the future?

what exactly have I got to offer?

Defining just what it is that you are going to put on the market cannot be done in isolation. You will also have to consider to whom, how, when, and where you are going to sell.

consider your product

If what you are going to sell is something produced by other people, for which you are going to act as retailer or middleman, agent or dealer you probably have no influence on the actual form of the product. The choice is between one brand and another, between the cheap and popular or the expensive and exclusive varieties of the product.

However, if it is something you have yourself produced, or designed (or had designed for you) and intend to produce, you can decide what the final form of the product will be. You can decide to produce it in several versions, with varying functions and at different price levels; you may make it highly specialised, with only one use, or you may incorporate several functions, in order to widen its appeal; or make it part of a range of related products; or change the materials of which it is made; or scrap it altogether and start again. Do not fall in love with the original idea and insist on going through with it, come hell or high water.

It may be unwise to include every possible refinement right from the start; a highly specialised product may appeal only to a small market. A simpler version may sell better and also pave the way for a more complex one, to be developed now and introduced at a later stage, incorporating new features in response to what were the first customers' reactions. (And if a *Which?* report says that the handle falls off, make sure you redesign it.)

If your product is more sophisticated than the prospective buyers are likely to demand, or too expensive for the ultimate consumer, you must simplify the product or decide to find another market for it, or produce two varieties for different types of user.

If the product requires the skills of several craftsmen, for example cabinet-maker and precision engineer, make sure from the start that you will have a supply of skilled labour to depend on. There is no use in building up a market for a product if you cannot maintain the supply. It might be better to design something that can be made by less skilled labour.

Ask yourself if the demand for your product is likely to be seasonal. A new nutcracker, for example, however super-efficient, is likely to sell readily only in the period before Christmas, so you may need another product (or several) to keep your plant and labour occupied for the rest of the year.

Where what you have to sell is quite simply a service plus your expertise, the need to define it precisely applies just as much as to a product. If, for example, you are setting up a security business, you should decide whether you are best able to supply a delivery service (complete with armoured cars), or human guards, or guard dogs, or specialist advice on how people can improve the security of their house or factory.

In the case of a consultancy or agency, too, define your scope as closely as possible, and relate it to your own experience. Rather than grandly planning to become an import-export agent, aim to trade with particular geographical areas and in specific products, preferably areas and products with which you are already familiar. When setting up as a consultant, you are more likely to succeed if you closely limit your field to where your particular expertise lies. Do not wait for your clients' reactions to tell you on what topics you are not qualified to give advice.

who are my customers and where shall I find them?

The nature of the product or service will dictate a general answer: woollen sweaters are for people, automated filing systems are for offices, easy-to-install damp-proof window frames should interest the building industry and the d-i-y enthusiast. A solar-panel water heating system may have limited use in England, but could be the basis of an export trade with sun-drenched countries.

Next, get some notion of how you should sell your products to your prospective customers, whether through a retail shop or a department store, through a wholesaler or by mail order, through agents or directly, in the UK or abroad.

some market research

Researching your market is not as formidable as it sounds. You yourself can do a lot of 'market research' from sources ready to hand, starting with public libraries.

The central library in your area should have a comprehensive reference department. In the commercial section of this you will find trade directories and publications relating to your business; Yellow Pages and telephone directories covering the whole country; directories of foreign importers; official digests of statistics, and much else.

Londoners are lucky: they command the superb resources of the Central Reference Library's commercial and technical section, but the chief town or city in your area should offer comparable facilities.

The Government Statistical Service makes available, on demand, a vast amount of information gathered by government departments, and by the Business Statistics Office and the Office of Population Censuses and Surveys. The booklet *Government Statistics: A Brief Guide to Sources* available free from the Press and Information Service, Central ▲ Statistical Service, Great George Street, London SW1P 3AQ, lists the various kinds of facts and figures available, and relates them to different aspects of business, such as marketing; the retail trade; external trade. Much of this is published in a series called *Business Monitors*.

Someone planning a comprehensive marketing strategy may want to study figures relating to national income and expenditure and population trends and projections. This may sound grandiose; what it amounts to is that you might get an idea of what proportion of what kind of people (teenagers, pensioners) is likely to want your product.

Some examples of where to find useful facts and figures include: *Classified List of Manufacturing Businesses* (issued in 10 parts), *Quarterly Statistics of Manufacturers' Sales, Population Trends* (quarterly), *Family Expenditure Survey* (annual), *Overseas Trade Statistics of the United Kingdom* (monthly), *Annual Statistics on Retail Trades*. You can ask for them at the public library; they are rather expensive.

Useful free publications, such as *Marketing: A Guide For Small Firms; How To Start Exporting; Selling To Large Firms* are available from the Small Firms Division of the Department of Industry, to which you

▲ can write at Abell House, John Islip Street, London SW1P 4LN. Or telephone (ask the operator for freefone 2444) to find out the address of your nearest Small Firms Centre, from which you can get much invaluable information.

trade organisations, trade journals, trade exhibitions

As a learner, you should snatch at every opportunity of consulting those who are already experts: your own trade organisation should be able to help you. Trade associations are listed in the Directory of British Associations (available in reference libraries). Journals and exhibitions will inform you about the prospects of your trade, future developments and new products, and will give you an idea who some of your potential buyers might be. The *Financial Times* publishes the dates of venues of forthcoming trade exhibitions. So, of course, does
▲ the *Exhibitions Bulletin* (266 Kirkdale, Sydenham, London SE26 4RZ; telephone: 01-778 2288).

If your product is to be sold to some trade or industry, you can use its trade directories to compile a list of potential customers.

You may find details of some more relevant journals and publications by looking at Brads Media Lists which are categorised by subject.

Chambers of Commerce and Chambers of Trade, besides being a source of information, may allow you access to their libraries.

Wherever economics or business studies are taught, at universities, polytechnics, local technical colleges, schools of business studies, you should be able to find a library, experts to consult, even students willing, for a modest fee, to do you market research for you. Make the arrangement, preferably in the autumn term, through the Management Studies or Trading Department.

dry run

This is something to attempt if you have started to manufacture your product in your spare time and are wondering whether to go into full production. Test your market for a small outlay, perhaps by distributing a few hundred leaflets, or putting a couple of dozen cards in shop windows. Do not distribute too many leaflets at a time, as you may not be able to deal with the number of requests: space out the distribution. This should give you some idea of whether anyone in the district is interested in what you have to offer.

who are my competitors?

The Yellow Pages will tell you what other similar businesses there are in your area, if you are counting on local trade.

Make yourself familiar with your competitors' products. Watch particularly for competitors' publicity and advertising: yours will have to be different and better. Send for their promotional literature and price lists, attend trade exhibitions. Trade directories and the trade press will give you relevant addresses.

If yours is a service industry, try approaching a similar firm for advice – but one operating in another area; you may find them remarkably willing to show you round their premises and answer questions. But do not expect your local firms to welcome and train more competition, and do not, in your enthusiasm, give your best ideas away to someone who may beat you to it.

If the competitor's product is one sold through retail outlets, go and see it at the point of sale to find out how it is displayed and promoted.

The object is to find out how your product would compare. Has it any unique features? Why should people prefer it to any other? What special features have the others products got, that could be incorporated in your product (with due regard to infringement of copyright or patents)? Something as simple as a hook, a lid, a heatproof base, could make all the difference to the appeal of a gadget.

how do I sell my products?

The actual business of putting anything on the market has several aspects including advertising, sales and distribution, pricing.

advertising and promotion

Which of the various media you should use for making your product known will depend very much on the nature of the product (or service), and how much you can afford.

The local press is particularly suited to a service or business which relies on local customers such as a plumber, electrician, hairdresser, launderette, flower shop. The cheapest advertisement is an insert in the classified advertisement section. This kind of advertisement does not catch the eye: it simply waits for someone looking for that type of service or product. So, to be effective, it should appear regularly.

If you want to catch the reader's passing glance, a display advertisement will be more effective or, if your budget permits, a larger, specially designed advertisement, placed on an editorial page (perhaps with a coupon on which further information can be requested, but then the return postage must be budgeted for). Such an advertisement, too, should appear regularly.

Many local papers undertake the design of a display advertisement but a professionally designed one is likely to be more eye catching. You can find a graphic designer through the Yellow Pages, but before commissioning him or her, make sure you know the cost.

Advertising in national newspapers and magazines is suited to a firm hoping to sell by mail order. It is essential to choose publications that are right for the type of goods – women's clothing in women's pages and magazines, sets of spanners in do-it-yourself magazines.

The trade press is the medium for goods that are sold not to individual consumers but to other firms. Much the same considerations apply as in the case of the national press; and where your advertisement is likely to appear cheek-by-jowl with those of competitors, it is essential to have an effective display that stands out, so professional advice is indicated. There are plenty of small local advertising agencies whose names can be found in the Yellow Pages or obtained from the Institute ▲ of Practitioners in Advertising (IPA), 44 Belgrave Square, London SW1 (telephone: 01-235 7020). Ask to see specimens of work and get an estimate before you engage one.

What you will be paying for is know-how – an agency should be able to design your advertising, advise on its content and wording, and place it in the appropriate media at the right times.

Trade exhibitions and local trade fairs have a triple function – for market research, for finding out what your competitors are producing, and also for selling your own goods to firms. They are not usually open to the general public. Your trade press will tell you where and when appropriate exhibitions are taking place, and where to apply to book space. There may be several suitable ones each year.

Exhibitions can be expensive; as well as hiring the stand, you must arrange for someone competent to be there to man it, explain and perhaps demonstrate your product, distribute literature and note down enquiries (to be scrupulously followed up). Probably that person will have to be you, with consequent loss of your valuable time. The exhibition should at least earn back its expenses eventually, so do not rush in too readily without thought and preparation.

You are more likely to attract the buyers' attention if you write to them beforehand, preferably by name (which you can find out by telephoning their firms). Send them your promotional literature and the number of your stand, and invite them to have a chat with you.

If you cannot afford a stand, or if your range of goods does not rate one, ask the Chamber of Commerce or your Small Business Club for the names of any other firms who might be willing to share a stand. Or you may be able to find out from the promoters of the exhibition the names of firms who are exhibiting related products; approach them to ask if they will lease you a share of their space and attendants.

If you sell to a wholesaler and he is exhibiting, he will probably show your product, anyway, and will only need a supply of promotional literature; or you may be able to organise a joint venture with one of your suppliers.

direct mail advertising

With direct mail advertising, you approach the customer directly, and by name. You send out a sales letter, accompanied by a leaflet, brochure or catalogue. The promotional literature should be designed to be eye-catching, by a professional, if possible. For the best effect, the advertising, the literature and the packaging should be co-ordinated.

making the most of the post

Contact your head postmaster if outside London, or district post master if in London for details of Freepost arrangements. All that the customer has to do, when there is a Freepost arrangement, is to add the words 'Freepost' prominently to the address he writes on the envelope, instead of sticking on the stamp. The address is a specially abbreviated one with a postcode given by the post office.

The charge is a ½p per item on top of ordinary second class postage. You have to pay a licence fee (at present £20 per annum) plus a minimum in advance (about £25 or some other appropriate amount), which is gradually used up as people write to you freepost. The post office send you weekly statements which will show when this float needs topping up.

The Post Office offers special terms to new firms embarking on direct mail operations: 1,000 first-class postings or 1,240 second-class ones completely free. There is also a bulk rate for large postings of pre-sorted letters. Further details can be obtained from the local Postal Services Representative (his number is in the telephone directory).

mailing lists

You do not, of course, write to the population at large; you need a mailing list of people likely to be interested.

If you want to sell to an industry or trade, you can make up your own mailing list out of entries in the trade directories; this is laborious but relatively inexpensive.

It is more effective if you can find out the name of each firm's buyer – from a trade reference book, the appropriate trade association or by telephoning the firm – and address the letter individually to him, making it appear unique. This is easy if you can get your letters prepared by a word processor (through a word processor bureau).

For advertising to local firms, relevant names and addresses from the Yellow Pages can be used in the same way.

For advertising to individual consumers, you can try to make up your own mailing list from the electoral register.

Many organisations have subscription or membership lists that they may be willing to rent out to you, for a fee. If the list is very large, they may agree to let you have part of it, or even just a very small part, so that you can test how well the list works for your purposes. Do not be too surprised, however, if the part that you are given for the test turns out to be the best part of the list. A large percentage of any full list is likely to be postally undeliverable – 'no such address' or 'gone away'.

You may be able to buy the list, in which case you will receive the names and addresses and can use them as often as you like, for whatever purpose you like. However, very few organisations sell their lists; they rather rent them out or exchange lists. Exchanging means that two organisations use each others' lists – but you, as a beginner, will not have anything to swop.

The organisation may make it a condition to have sight of and approve the offer which is to be mailed. To prevent you from copying their lists, they may insist that the addressing and posting are done by a specialist mailing company.

You will, of course, learn the names and addresses of those who reply, and they then become part of your own list, which you later may sell, rent out or exchange. There are a number of list brokers who may be able to help you find lists, for a fee.

counting the cost

But first calculate the likely cost, and be clear how to assess the responses. 25p per name and address may not sound very much, but if the response rate is one per cent, the cost becomes £25 per reply.

The response rate to direct mail advertising is variable, depending on the product, the market and the care taken in preparation: a 3–5 per cent response should be considered as extremely good. Naturally, not every enquiry results in an order; after your first mail shot you should be able to calculate whether the resulting business has earned back its promotion costs plus some profit.

Leaflet distribution is a humbler, localised version of direct mail. At its simplest, this could be a leaflet pushed through a few hundred neighbourhood doors by hired teenages or an active retired person. You may be able to arrange for the newsagent to slip a leaflet inside every newspaper delivered, for a fee.

If you want to cover larger or more distant areas, you would have to entrust the work to a specialist firm: look in the Yellow Pages under Addressing and Circularising Services, and Circular and Sample Distributors.

press releases

Any event of special interest in your firm – the opening of a new workshop or the launching of a new product – should be communicated to the local and trade press, in the form of a press release. Do not be intimidated by 'press release' – all you have to do is find out who is in charge of the, say, technical page of the newspaper and then write to them with a suitable small article. Make sure that the relevant details are there of the product and of yourself, your name, your address, the prices. The better and more straightforwardly it is written, the more likely it is to get in. Pictures help, but they should be black and white. If what you send catches editorial attention, and secures a paragraph or two of editorial copy, this is often more effective than any advertisement. If you place an advertisement at the same time, you may get editorial mention – but the two are not invariably linked.

To get mentioned in the national press is helpful for anyone selling by mail order. Try to think who would be interested in your story, such as the women's page editor, perhaps.

selling

You will need to consider the question of distribution and selling long before you can manufacture enough to satisfy widespread demand.

selling to shops

At the most basic level, this is a question of taking round a sample of your product to appropriate shops in the district and persuading them to stock it. To go about this sensibly,

- make an appointment to see the shop's owner or manager; do not simply turn up unannounced at the busiest time
- make yourself familiar with competing products, their prices and their drawbacks, so that you can point out the advantages of yours (without obvious knocking)
- be clear about the price of your product, but be willing to allow the retailer an attractive discount. The real problem is to decide whether to sell on sale or return, or not. On the whole, it is better not to, but if you find that one particular line does not move and others do, you could offer to buy it back in order to get the shop to take more of the stuff that does sell
- be prepared to prove that you can guarantee supplies and will stick to delivery dates
- have the product or range of your products properly packaged, as it will look when displayed in a window or shelf
- Sometimes it also helps to offer a small display aid, to show your product to its best advantage. Make clear to the shop owner that this is on loan to display your product, not a gift, nor for use to show off someone else's goods.

The technique for larger shops, or chain stores, is to start by contacting the appropriate buyer in each store. The retail directory (from a reference library) gives some names; find out others by telephoning. Make an appointment to see each buyer.

- Pay particular attention to the presentation of your product.
- Know your maximum capacity and the size of orders you can guarantee to deliver and your most dependable delivery dates.
- Be prepared to prove that you can finance your increased output.

- When you come to discuss the price, be sure to have some room for negotiating. But remember, some large shops will expect extended credit terms and will delay payment.

Most large companies pay on a 30-day account: that is, they pay invoices on their first accounting day occurring when 30 days have passed from receipt of the invoice. (That is why it is important to invoice customers promptly and correctly, offering no excuse for delaying payment).

If you negotiate a major contract, ask for stage payments: for instance, part payment with the order and then percentage payments at various stages of production or delivery.

pricing

The price you charge for a product or service can be arrived at in various ways. Economists have theories about price based on cost, based on competition, based on the demand, based on the going rate; in real life for the small businessman, these categories tend to slide into each other.

Pricing based on costs is a crude but still commonly used method. The price is made up of the cost of the product to the manufacturer (labour, materials, overheads) plus a percentage mark-up to give what you consider to be a fair profit.

This method, however, ignores two important factors: demand and competition. Unless you are selling bread during a famine, demand will set an upper limit on what you can charge, and so will the presence in the market of competitors; and your own costs will set the lower limit.

You must allow for discounts for quantity orders, or for payment in seven days and for anything else that might encourage greater purchase or quicker settlement.

If you sell to the final consumer, by retail or through mail order, there is no problem with getting payment; but if you sell to another firm, you may well need to offer credit – because the competition does – and you must cost that in.

If you sell through a wholesaler, your price must allow for the wholesaler's and retailer's profit as well as your own. The price to the customer will contain the three elements of the wholesaler's mark-up, the retailer's mark-up and your profit (plus VAT if applicable). You must allow for these in order not to price yourself out of the market.

pricing based on competition

It is important to identify your competitors and to make yourself familiar with what they are offering at what prices. In pricing a product you can, to a large extent, be guided by what competitors are asking for a comparable product.

For most products there are several price ranges, and manufacturers deliberately tailor their goods to fit into one of these. Some manufacturers produce several product ranges, each one for a different category. Cosmetics, for instance, tend to be cheap and cheerful for the young, medium priced for the average user, and extremely expensive for the richer consumer. You should decide at an early stage into which price category your product will slot.

If you cannot fit into the lower or middle range, because your costs are irreducibly high, you will have to aim at the higher category: but then you will have to make sure that the prices reflect some special and unique quality of your goods, and show the customer that this is so. There are some categories of goods – cosmetics, again, are an example – where a high price can actually be a selling point: the customer is reassured by it that she is getting a unique, luxury article, and it would be an error of psychology to charge less.

Another way of taking demand into account is this. If you produce a range of related goods, some will be more in demand than others: your pricing should therefore be based on a profit margin averaged out over the whole range.

Or you may try loss-leader pricing of one or more items, at cost, or very little above it, as a bait to capture a large share of the market quickly. But you will be the baiter bit if you sell all the low-profit items and none of the high-profit ones.

Pricing based on the going rate incorporates the elements of competition and of demand. It is the way of pricing that obtains in most service industries. Where there is no going rate, you must cost your own time very carefully when calculating your overheads. But usually, there is a recognised going rate for the service, and in order to charge more, you would need to offer something out of the ordinary: such as being on call at all hours, or having unusually high qualifications, or offering a particularly comprehensive service.

face-to-face selling

Many people who would find no difficulty in selling goods across a shop counter, feel deeply embarrassed when it comes to calling on firms to offer their goods or services.

In fact, aggressive selling is seldom required: one's best weapon is a detailed knowledge of one's project and a readiness to explain it fluently, even demonstrate it.

Present as good an appearance as possible: as a small entrepreneur, you will inspire more confidence by a show of frugal efficiency than by lavish trimmings. (For some kinds of service only, such as consultancy perhaps, appearances are important, since you may have nothing else to show your client.)

Keep good records of your customers – how much they buy and when – and keep in constant touch, so that when they think of buying, you are in the forefront of their minds. Ask them if they are satisfied, and treat complaints in a friendly spirit; look into the complaint and put right anything that needs rectifying.

Genuinely listen to what the potential customer says, and show an obvious interest in what he or she wants.

In many cases you must be able to offer a service, as well as a product: installation, spare parts and servicing. Make sure that you have the facilities for this, or next time the customer may go elsewhere. If you cannot provide the service yourself, find a sub-contractor.

Know your potential customer's own products and be able to discuss them intelligently, and if you yourself happen to use his competitor's product, keep this to yourself.

employing an agent

If you dislike or have no talent for selling, or do not have time for it, you may be better occupied concentrating on the production side, while getting someone else to sell for you. You might think of persuading a golden-tongued friend to do you the favour, if only for the initial contacting, but a proper business partner, or, best of all for this purpose, a proper agent, is preferable.

The advantages for a new business can be considerable. An agent will have the necessary contacts, and be known in the trade; he can also keep you informed about what your competitors are doing. He will need to be primed with any necessary technical information and supplied with promotional literature, possibly backed with advertising.

The disadvantage is that the agent's commission reduces your profit margin – but perhaps you would not have had the profit at all, but for him.

An agent usually represents more than one firm, and you can never be sure that he is trying as hard for you as for the others: he naturally works hardest for products offering the highest return.

To find an agent, consult one or all of these: the trade press; trade directories; Yellow Pages (under Manufacturers' Agents and Marketing Consultants); or advertise for one yourself. You can negotiate any agreement that seems suitable, but both the agent and you must be quite clear about the terms before he starts.

Mail order selling

Direct response mail order selling is a system in which press advertisements urge customers to order goods, which are then sent to them directly.

Payment is usually by cash (cheque) with order or by credit card; it is usual to offer free approval ('money back if not delighted') which is required by most of the relevant codes of practice; some firms offer credit terms, but these are usually catalogue mail order houses rather than firms selling their own products.

To be suitable for mail order selling, the product should fall into one or more of these categories:

- Light in weight and strong enough not to break in transit.
- Or else bulky, but capable of being compactly and securely packed – many types of garden sheds and greenhouses are sold by mail order.
- Not obtainable in ordinary retail shops, that is, in some way new, unique or hard to find – for example a craft product, or something for a minority taste.
- Or obtainable in shops, but at a much higher price. Make sure, however, that the customer's postage costs do not take away your price advantage. Because of postage, very low-priced articles are not worth selling by mail.

Your customers must be left in no doubt about the total cost of any goods offered. In particular, make it clear whether the costs of packing and postage or delivery are included in the price, and if not, what these costs are.

Not only your production but your packing, despatch and administration must be up to scratch. Before starting the operation, be sure that you have the stocks and the extra capacity to meet a sudden increase in demand, and are able to deliver goods within the promised period. This should be within 28 days unless you have made quite clear in the advertisement when you will be despatching (perhaps 'in time for Christmas'). If you suddenly find that an order cannot be sent off within the period you promised, you should immediately contact the buyer and offer a refund.

These points, and very many others with which you must comply in this form of selling, are contained in the code of practice of the British ▲ Direct Marketing Association Ltd, 1 New Oxford Street, London WC1 A1NQ (telephone: 01-242 2254). The Mail Order Trader's Association, ▲ 507 Corn Exchange Building, Fenwick Street, Liverpool L2 7RA (telephone: 051-236 7581), has its own code of practice which applies to catalogue mail trading. The members of that association sell through catalogues issued to agents or directly to the general public by post.

You must conform to both the legal requirements and the voluntary codes of practice governing mail order selling. And to advertise in the national press, you must get clearance from the Newspaper Publishers' Association and pay an annual fee to a fund which indemnifies readers against loss due to a firm's failure to supply goods ordered. Similar schemes are operated by many local papers and magazines. Advertising in the classified column is exempt from the NPA's stipulation, but you still have to get your advertising copy cleared. It must, in any event, conform to the Advertising Standards Authority's code. The ASA's ▲ address is Brook House, Todington Place, London WC1 (telephone: ▲ 01-580 5555), and that of the Newspaper Publishers' Association is 6 Bouverie Street, London EC4 (telephone: 01-583 8132).

Make sure that you have an efficient system for recording the name and address of each customer (which is then added to your own mailing list), the product bought, and the dates of purchase and despatch.

As with direct mail advertising, ask the postal services representative about reduced terms for bulk parcel despatch; this is done on a contract basis.

If you advertise in several newspapers and magazines, it is worth using a simple code to distinguish replies from each source, so that you can tell which one brings in the most business.

The price you charge for your product must take into account the advertising costs – often as much as $\frac{1}{3}$ of the selling price – as well as the cost of replacing damaged articles, and, if you offer credit, of bad debts. If you sell on credit, or free approval, allow for this in your cash flow forecasting.

Providing credit card facilities may be worth while, since it allows the customer to obtain credit without risk to yourself – your money is guaranteed.

To become a credit card agent, you have to approach the area sales office of the credit card organisation and within about ten days a representative will call to make the arrangements. There is a service charge or commission of around 5 per cent (which is sometimes changed).

Because in mail order selling there is no customer's signature on the credit card slip, you have to enter the details (customer's card number and its expiry date, the name and address, amount charged) and send this schedule to the headquarters of the card company. You must not despatch the goods until you have the headquarters' authorisation. Your account will be credited with the amount, minus the service charge or commission.

selling in a very small way

Market stalls and country fairs provide an outlet for a small business making a slow, cautious start at selling, and are particularly suited to craft goods. The local authority who do the licensing of stalls will be able to tell you where and when fairs are held in the district, and how to rent a stall, either permanently or by the day.

Exhibiting at a local craft fair could be a good way of launching a product; the tourist boards in England, Scotland and Wales have lists of all the craft and country fairs in Britain. Some craft associations, whose addresses you can find in the annual *Craftsman's Directory*, Brook House, Mint Street, Godalming, Surrey, GU7 1HE (telephone: 04868 22184), will arrange to exhibit members' work.

Premises

The question of premises obviously varies according to the type of business. The kind of space you need to work in will depend largely on whether you manufacture goods, or sell them, or offer a service.

premises for a service industry

If you provide a service, for example as a builder, decorator, plumber, probably all of your work will be carried on in your customers' premises. To begin with, you will only need some space at home in which to do the paperwork, and perhaps a shed or garage for storing tools. However, if your business thrives and grows, and you come to employ workmen, you will eventually need an office to deal with enquiries, estimates and paperwork, and also larger storage space, and parking for your vans – proper business premises, in fact.

If your business is a consultancy or agency needing little or no equipment, you may require only a room or two, and may find it convenient to make over some part of your house to business use, or you may choose to rent a small office somewhere else. The physical location of your office may not be crucial to your success.

Obviously, for a very small and new business there is a tremendous advantage in working from home: you save on rent, rates, cost of the public utilities, cleaning – and even staff, if a member of your family answers the door and the telephone and perhaps does the typing.

However, some house deeds prohibit use for business purposes, and most restrictive covenants of this type would be enforceable. Even where there are no such restrictions, if you carry on a business from residential premises, you may need planning permission from the local authority, and may have to pay higher rates for commercial occupation. You should, in any event, inform the company who is insuring your house. Using it for business, particularly if you are storing any combustible goods, may invalidate the buildings and contents insurance – even against totally unrelated disasters, such as a burst water pipe.

There are plenty of small businessmen who work inconspicuously from home without permission and get away with it, because there is nothing in their work to inconvenience the neighbours or alert snoopers. But if you want to be above-board in carrying on your business, or if your house needs to be altered in any way for the purpose, as in adding a room or shed, you must apply for permission. There is a fee, at present £44, payable when an application for planning permission for a change in the use of a building is submitted to the local authority.

If your work does not annoy the other residents or change the character of the street, you may well succeed. Remember the potential capital gains tax liability on the portion of your home used for business, if you come to sell the house.

The permission may be qualified by some conditions relating to hours of work, or callers at the house. If your application is refused, you have the right to appeal, but if this fails, you may have no choice but to look for outside accommodation.

premises for a manufacturing business

Unless you are a craftsman working single-handed and in a very small way of business, it is unlikely that you will be able to work from home: apart from probable lack of workshop space, you will run into opposition from the local authority.

A manufacturing firm has to satisfy zoning regulations for light and heavy industry, because it may create noise, smoke, fumes, industrial waste that must be disposed of, other sorts of environmental pollution; or it may increase the risk of fire. It is extremely unlikely that you could carry on a manufacturing business clandestinely, or that you would get permission to do so in residential premises.

As for renting workshop space, at the present time there are many millions of square feet of factory premises vacant in Britain, but only a small percentage of this is suitable for a company just starting in business. Just the same, there is no reason why you should not get hold of some of this percentage if you go about it the right way.

hunting for workshop space

Define your exact requirements. You will need a site big enough to allow your firm to settle down and expand, because you may not want to have to move in a year or two. There must be access to all the mains services; warehousing space; room and amenities for the work-people; parking space; room for lorries to load and unload. You probably do not need a central situation or a street frontage, but you must ensure that any noise, fumes, smoke, do not annoy people living nearby, especially during overtime working.

You may need an office, if you expect customers to be calling on you. There may be a number of other requirements: it is unlikely that one site will satisfy all of them.

Begin by applying to the local authority. Some authorities try to cater for the very small business by building 'nursery' units, which are simply shells, sometimes only 500 square feet (about the size of a double garage). The cost of building these is high, and so, consequently are the rents. But, if the authority is anxious to promote employment, it may offer you a short period rent-free.

The local authority may give you favourable rental terms, or even a rent-free period, if they want you out of a mainly residential area where you activities are unwelcome and you are what they call a 'non-conformer user', and the neighbours (can be persuaded to) campaign for your removal or closure.

Some councils keep a register of vacant industrial property, and may be able to help you by extracting from this a list of suitable properties. Most local authorities recognise that their attitude to small business can affect unemployment levels, and are as helpful as they can be.

But if official bodies cannot help, you must make the rounds of the estate agents. If you do resort to these, remember that they may need telephoning at intervals to remind them of your existence. Low-cost, low-rental premises have little value to an agent because they bring in a low fee. Very small and cheap premises in the centre of town do not always reach the estate agents' lists, so keep your own eyes open, and also study the classified advertisements in the local press.

When you find a place that seems suitable, there are still a number of factors to be considered, for instance, whether to buy or to lease. Most people starting a small business are likely to want to keep their capital readily available rather than sink it in buying property (and mortgage repayments can be a burden). So you would be well advised to rent premises in the first instance, on as short a lease as possible, and so minimise your responsibilities until you are confident of success.

However, you should be assured of having the option of renewing the lease, and for a longer period, otherwise you may have to move just when you least want to.

It is unwise to rent or buy a building without having a survey done; you might have unpleasant surprises later, when structural or other faults may come to light. If the survey sounds expensive, talk to the surveyor about a negotiated fee. You do not want a lengthy catalogue listing features that you can see for yourself, nor a full unlimited guarantee on which you could sue if he missed anything. What you want is a realistic guide to the value of the property and what you must do to it soon, what you can risk leaving for a while, and what is unimportant structurally. Such information is as useful given orally as it would be in a typed document, and is far cheaper, especially if it is without the insurance-underwritten indemnity.

If the property is and older one which you will have to refurbish at your own expense, you will be increasing its value to the owner, so you may be able to negotiate a cheaper rent.

Check that there will be no difficulties with the mains services, that there will be enough electric power, water, gas, and also adequate drainage, and no difficulties about the telephone.

Somebody who is a low user of water should ask the water undertaking or water authority to be allowed to be metered instead of being charged a fixed rate.

fire prevention

Premises require a fire certificate if they are used as a place of work, a shop, factory or office where more than 20 people are employed, or more than 10 people elsewhere than on the ground floor; or if explosives or highly inflammable substances are stored there.

If you are moving into previously occupied premises, find out whether there is a current fire certificate, and if so, whether it covers your operations. Your occupancy may constitute a change of conditions because of structural alterations, a change of use, or change in the number of persons working: if so, you will need a new certificate.

Your local fire prevention officer grants the certificate if he is satisfied, after inspecting the premises, that all necessary precautions have been taken.

Consult your fire prevention officer before you clinch the deal for any premises: if your work means installing a number of fire escapes, fire doors, new flooring, this may prove to be too expensive to be worth-while. You cannot argue with a fire prevention officer: his word is law with no appeal, and he can close you down without notice.

Even if you do not need a fire certificate, your premises must have adequate means of escape, and fire-fighting equipment.

planning permission

Unless the premises you choose have already been in industrial use, you will need the permission of the local authority's planning department for a 'change of use'.

If you take the local authority's planners into your confidence from the start, they may prove remarkably helpful, and eager not to thwart a new business, unless there are overwhelming objections to the plans you put forward.

If you intend to start from a green field site and build on it, planning permission will take much longer, and is only one of the obstacles to be overcome.

rates and concessions

If you are not tied to any one area and can set up anywhere, you may do best in an assisted area, where you may sometimes get rent-free accommodation for up to two years, perhaps in a purpose-built factory.

In assisted areas, particularly where jobs are clearly going to be created, the Department of Industry can provide factory units, rent-free for the intitial period. Many local authorities – yours may be one of them – are prepared to give intitial rate relief to new businesses, and those relocating themselves into the area. Get in touch with the planning department or the economic unit of your local authority about these or other concessions.

If you intend to set up businesses in a rural area, consult the local CoSIRA office which may know of small properties, converted barns, or other accommodation available for rent.

sublet premises

If you need only a modest amount of space, you may be able to find an existing business which has spare capacity, and is glad to reduce its overheads by subletting to you.

The kind of business to look for is one in a similar but not competing line of business: the association could even result in a partnership.

Squaring up to accounts

The figures that your business generates are an index of its health and growth. Many people in a small business seem to be positively scared of them and keep no continuous control.

It is not good enough to monitor the state of health of the business by the annual accounts, which are not available until the following year is well advanced. If anything is then found to be amiss, it may well be too late to put it right.

You may feel that, if you employ an accountant, it is his business to keep an eye on the figures on the why-keep-a-dog-and-bark-yourself? principle. But an accountant should rather be thought of as a doctor: he cannot compel you to look after your business health properly, he can only diagnose the sickness resulting from your imprudence, and he certainly cannot cure it once it has become terminal.

So, do not be scared of your accounts and take an informed interest in what the figures show you.

You should know at the end of each month, if not every week, whether it has been a profitable one, and whether you have enough money in hand or on tap, to cover your expenses for the coming month. Your calculations need not be very elaborate: quite rough monthly accounts, backed up by an accountant's quarterly report, will enable you to stay in control.

what you can do for yourself

Your accountant could, of course, carry out your monthly monitoring for you; but it is most unlikely that your new, small, business could afford the expense. If you do this work for yourself, you will be in a position to know, at all times, what is happening to your business, and to forecast what is going to happen next.

What is more, you will then have no trouble in understanding the accountant's quarterly reports, and relating them to your own day-to-day experience. Even if you prefer to have your accountant do all the figure work, you must be able to make sense of the reports he prepares for you.

keeping business records

There are excellent reasons why you should keep good business records: because the Inland Revenue and Customs and Excise (for VAT) require it, and because you will save your accountant's time (which he charges for by the hour). But the most important reason is that properly kept accounts, summarised at the end of each month and coupled with a stocktake or an estimate of the value of your stock, will give you the up-to-date knowledge of your affairs which you need to spot danger signs while there is still time to put things right.

who keeps the books?

Although all modern double-entry book-keeping follows the same general pattern, no two firms' sets of books are identical: every business has some individual aspects which must be recorded, and every businessman has his own notions of which of these records he needs to monitor.

So get your accountant, who understands your particular requirements, to set up your books for you, and to teach you how to keep them. He will probably do so willingly, for it is to his advantage, as well as yours, to be presented with clear, well-kept books to deal with. Or, better still, ask him to teach some member of your family whom you can conscript to relieve you of the task. It is not difficult, and it will probably be some time before your business demands the services of a fulltime trained book-keeper.

You can also teach yourself the elements of book-keeping from one of a variety of books on the subject, but be sure to acquire this skill before you start up, because you certainly will not have time afterwards.

the records you must keep

Business records may be kept and presented in a variety of ways, and depend very much on the type of business for their format.

However, one feature is common to all systems: they must be backed by evidence that the receipts and payments recorded have actually been made. So be sure to keep safely all of the following:

- cheque-book stubs
- cancelled cheques (tell the bank to return them to you)
- bank paying-in books (use them, not paying-in slips)
- bank statements (make sure that you have separate accounts – even if they are at the same bank – for business and private life, whether you are sole trader or partnership or company)
- copies of your own invoices, receipts and delivery notes
- your suppliers' invoices, receipts and delivery notes
- receipts, wherever possible, for minor expenditure made in cash.

the books

For keeping accounts, even at their simplest, you must keep several books.

The cash book is the most basic account book: it records all your payments and receipts made by cheque (for this purpose cheques are regarded as cash) or in ready money.

Some businesses are purely cash ones – that means that, whether you are buying or selling, payment is made immediately. If yours is not one of these, and you buy and sell with payment at a later date, you will need two further books, a sales day book for recording your sales invoices as they are sent out, and a purchases day book in which are recorded your purchases of goods and services.

This last book, which is all-important, will be of the kind called an analysis book, ruled with a number of vertical columns, in which you classify your different kinds of expenditure: materials, direct labour and the various sorts of overheads. Be sure to get a book with enough columns: how many you will need depends on your particular expenses, and on how minutely you want to break them down.

By adding up each column every month, you will see exactly how much each of your business expenses came to; the total of these totals will give you your whole month's costs.

If you are registered for VAT, you will have a VAT column in both your sales and your purchases books, to record the amount of VAT that other people pay you, and that which you pay: this information you will need for your quarterly VAT return.

If you employ anyone, you must keep a record of wages paid, showing gross earnings, deductions for income tax, National Insurance, any pension scheme, any other deductions, net pay and the employer's National Insurance contributions.

The petty cash book is a record of small out-of-pocket expenses paid by you or your staff in the course of work. It may include any number of different things, such as fares, taxis, the window-cleaner and the tea bought for tea-breaks. The money is paid out of a float drawn at intervals from the bank (and duly recorded in the cash and purchase books). The petty cash book is on the same lines as the purchases book, with columns for different sorts of expenditure.

slightly more advanced book-keeping

As your business expands and becomes more complex, you will need to start keeping ledgers.

The sales ledger is based on the sales day book, and records the individual accounts of each of your customers, showing how much he has bought in any given period and the date of his payments. This enables you to keep an eye on slow payers. (It is also invaluable in planning future marketing strategy. It may show, for instance, that 80 per cent of your trade is with a few customers placing substantial orders, and 20 per cent is with a large number of small customers. You will then have to decide whether to go on accepting small orders whose costs are high in relation to the profits, in the hope that the small customers may be encouraged to grow into bigger ones.)

The purchases ledger is based on the purchases day book, and records your transactions with each of your suppliers. It shows which of them are getting the largest share of your custom; these will be the ones most likely to give credit or offer generous cash discounts.

The general ledger records impersonal payments, that is the sale and purchase of equipment, rent and rates, services, etc, and the totals of income and expenditure.

These ledgers are the foundation for a double entry book-keeping system. A full explanation of this would require a book to itself, but the principle on which it is based is a simple one: it is that every transaction must be recorded twice, once as a debit and once as a credit, according to whether it is regarded from a buyer's or a seller's point of view.

Every sale you make represents a debit entry to your customer in the sales ledger and a credit to you in the sales account in the general ledger: when the customer pays, this appears as a debit entry in the cash book and a credit entry in the sales ledger.

Every purchase you make from your supplier is a credit entry for him in your purchases ledger and a debit for you in the general ledger. When you pay up, this is recorded as a credit in your cash book and a debit for the supplier in the purchases ledger.

using what your figures tell you

With all these records you are in a position to make calculations showing how your business is progressing. The all-important one is your monthly net profit. To arrive at this, you need to draw up a monthly trading account and a profit and loss account. The monthly trading account shows the gross profits of your business. You calculate it by adding together your month's labour and materials costs, and the difference between the value of your opening and closing stocks, and subtracting this from the total monthly sales figure.

Bill's product sells at £20 per unit; of this, his materials cost £10, and labour additional to his own, costs £2. His overheads, averaged out, are £800 a month. Using the sales, purchase and labour totals shown by his books, Bill draws up a trading account, thus:

BILL'S TRADING ACCOUNT FOR ONE MONTH

	£		£
Opening stock		Sales	4,000
(100 units @ £12)	1,200		
Purchases of materials			
(200 @ £10)	2,000		
Labour (200 @ £2)	400		
	3,600		
Less closing stock			
(100 @ £12)	1,200		
	2,400		
Balance, i.e. gross profit	1,600		
	4,000		4,000

Bill has valued his stock at materials and labour costs only: overheads do not enter the calculation until the next step, the monthly estimated net profit. This is how it looks in Bill's case:

BILL'S PROFIT AND LOSS ACCOUNT

	£		£
Overheads	800	Gross profit	1,600
Balance, i.e. net profit	800		
	1,600		1,600

This is the most basic way of drawing up a profit and loss account. It can, in fact, be combined with the trading account in a single calculation. There is no special presentation that must be followed.

You can make it more informative by making it more complex: you can isolate and thus spotlight items of overheads or other factors that you particularly want to keep an eye on, for instance, the cost of the power consumption. Or, because power is a cost that varies with the volume of production, you could choose to treat it as a materials purchase, rather than an overhead.

Here we have assumed that Bill's enterprise is a limited company and his salary is therefore one of the overheads. If he were a sole trader, his remuneration (say, £400 a month) would not be included in the overheads, which would then be £400 a month, and the month's net profit before tax would be £1,200, and would constitute Bill's taxable income.

However, you may have a profit and loss account that looks as healthy as this one, and still run out of funds, because it does not show that at any one time you may not actually have in hand all the money due to you. If your suppliers demand cash on delivery while your customers will only place orders on 30 or 60 day credit terms, and your expanding business is demanding additional unforeseen expenditure, you have got a cash flow problem.

cash flow forecasting

Bill's latest cash flow forecast looked like this (figures in brackets denote a deficit):

Month	Jan.	Feb.	Mar.	Apr.	May
	£	£	£	£	£
Opening bank balance/(overdraft)	(3,000)	(2,200)	(1,400)	(600)	200
Payments:					
purchases	2,000	2,000	2,000	2,000	2,000
labour	400	400	400	400	400
overheads	800	800	800	800	800
Maximum borrowing requirement	6,200	5,400	4,600	3,800	3,000
Receipts from sales	4,000	4,000	4,000	4,000	4,000
Closing balance/(overdraft)	(2,200)	(1,400)	(600)	200	1,000

Bill is now asked to take on a regular order for another 200 units a months, but with payment only after 90 days. This means another machine at £500, plus additional part-time labour costs, and it will take two months to build up the manufacturing capacity. In order to be in a position to decide whether to accept the order, Bill prepares another forecast, which looks like this:

CASH FLOW FORECAST II
(figures in brackets denote a deficit)

Month	Jun.	July	Aug.	Sept.	Oct.	Nov.	Dec.
Products made	200	300	400	400	400	400	400
	£	£	£	£	£	£	£
Opening balance/(overdraft)	1,000	300	(1,300)	(2,900)	(4,500)	(4,100)	(1,700)
Payments:							
purchases	3,000	4,000	4,000	4,000	4,000	4,000	4,000
wages	400	800	800	800	800	800	800
overheads	800	800	800	800	800	800	800
Capital expenditure	500						
Maximum borrowing requirement	3,700	5,300	6,900	8,500	10,100	9,700	7,300
Receipts from sales	4,000	4,000	4,000	4,000	6,000	8,000	8,000
Closing balance/(overdraft)	300	(1,300)	(2,900)	(4,500)	(4,100)	(1,700)	700

It shows him that if he accepts the order under these conditions, he will need a further investment of around £4,500 for 3 months, to pay for the additional costs. The bank might well be willing, on the basis of this profitable order, to lend the money to a customer who had already succeeded in repaying an overdraft of £3,000. To minimise his borrowing requirement, Bill might be able to persuade his suppliers to agree to a delayed payment, and might also be able to dovetail this payment into those months when no major overheads were due. VAT payments (here excluded for the sake of simplicity), even though later refunded, would adversely affect the cash flow.

In order to keep the example simple, two other factors have been excluded: the cost of additional power consumption resulting from increased production, and the interest payable on bank loans or overdrafts; but a rough calculation is all that is wanted at this stage.)

Bill's experience shows that for a small, newly-established firm, a large order, unaccompanied by prompt payment, can be a disaster if there is no means of stretching resources to cover the expenditure demanded by the additional output. By making a forecast on similar lines, you will be able to see how your money supply will relate to your expenditure.

Having discovered what your volume of production is to be in the next six months, or so, your next task is to discover at which point you will begin to make a profit.

break-even point

Every business has a break-even point, at which it is producing just enough for the receipts to balance the costs. Before this point is reached, it is working at a loss; when it is passed, the business is showing a profit.

In a manufacturing business, the break-even point is measured in units of production; in a service one, in the number of paid hours worked.

fixed and variable costs

The costs of manufacturing anything can be divided into two categories: fixed and variable.

The fixed costs are the ones which remain the same whatever the amount you manufacture: the overheads, and in the short term, labour. The variable costs, which vary with the amount you manufacture, are materials and power. (In the example which follows, power, for simplicity's sake, has been left as an overhead.)

In Bill's case, the relationship between his volume of production (number of units made) and his profitability is as follows:

Units made	Variable cost	Fixed cost	Total cost	Receipts from sales	Profit/ (loss)
20	200	1,200	1,400	400	(1,000)
60	600	1,200	1,800	1,200	(600)
100	1,000	1,200	2,200	2,000	(200)
140	1,400	1,200	2,600	2,800	200

These figures can be expressed in a graph. The horizontal axis represents the number of units produced, the vertical axis represents money: on this are plotted Bill's selling price and total cost at each volume of production. The two lines intersect at the point at which production is 120 units: this is where he is just covering his costs, and beyond this, he will begin to make a profit.

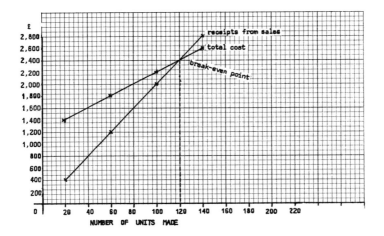

A calculation and simple graph like this will enable you to plan your volume of production intelligently in relation to your financial resources.

balance sheet

At any time after starting up, you may want to analyse your deployment of your resources: the balance sheet constitutes such an analysis.

It shows the financial state of the firm at a given time – usually the end of the trading year – and is based on the account balances in the ledgers.

It takes account not only of outgoings and receipts but of what the business owns (its assets), and of what it owes (its liabilities). Both of these may be subdivided into fixed and current ones.

– *Fixed liabilities* are debts which are repayable over a long period of time.

– *Current liabilities* are those which must be repaid in the short term, such as debts to suppliers, overdrafts, and interest on loans.

– *Fixed assets* are property such as land, buildings, plant, machinery and vehicles. (These need to be revalued periodically, and their book value adjusted; land and buildings tend to increase in value with inflation, while plant, machinery and vehicles depreciate and have to be replaced. It is useful to set up a sinking fund or reverse for an eventual replacement cost.)

– *Current assets* include customers' book debts, the value of any stock held, and money in hand or in the bank.

In Bill's case, his resources have been as follows: £3,000 capital; an overdraft facility of £2,000, of which he is at present using only £1,200; a medium-term bank loan of £2,500 to buy plant and machinery. His profit has not been taken out, but kept in reserve to be used to buy additional plant and to provide additional working capital. The astute businessman would invest his reserves, if these were not needed immediately, which would then be entered as 'investments' on the asset side of the balance.

Bill's balance sheet might look like this:

	£	
Fixed assets:		
plant and machinery	6,500	
motor vehicles	4,000	
	10,500	
less hire-purchase debt	2,000	
		8,500
Current assets:		
stock	1,000	
debtors	2,500	
	3,500	
less current liabilities		
creditors	2,800	
overdraft	1,200	
Net current assets/(liabilities)		(500)
Total net assets		8,000

The resources to generate these assets are:

	£
Capital	3,000
Loan	2,500
Reserves	2,500
Total	8,000

There are other ways of presenting a balance sheet, and individual items can be more closely analysed; for instance, stock can be divided into finished stock and raw materials. If you are making your balance sheet, keep it simple to begin with; if an accountant does it for you, be sure that he does it in a form that you can understand.

The very basic balance sheet shown above does not take account of the difference between a sole trader (or partnership) and a limited company. In actual practice, the balance sheet of a company would have to be drawn up rather differently. Its capital would have to be shown among the liabilities, because it belongs, not to the company, but to its shareholders. The same is true of the net profit on the trading account: it must ultimately be distributed among the shareholders. In a sole-trader firm or partnership, the capital investment and the profits are owned by the firm and are, therefore, assets.

factoring

If you are in real cash flow trouble, perhaps because you have reached your bank borrowing limit and have a lot of customers owing you money which they are in no hurry to pay, you could possibly resort to factoring. The factoring company advances you the money owing on your customers' invoices, and retains a percentage as commission when they are paid.

Consult your bank manager for the name of a suitable company. Most factoring companies are backed by clearing banks or other major financial organisations. One disadvantage is that they often take only those firms which have a turnover in excess of a set (very high) amount.

It is an expensive way of buying money and only to be resorted to if things are – temporarily – desperate, not as a standard way of bridging the gap between outgoings and receipts, or to ensure that slow paying customers do not lock up your working capital.

As a rule of trading, you should do all you can to induce those who owe you money to pay as quickly as possible, while paying your own bills with as much delay as possible. In both cases, the discount for quick payment is at stake; you must either give it to your customers or forfeit it from your suppliers. But in any event, a cash discount given or forfeited is likely to cost considerably less than the factoring commission.

Taxation and the small business

When you set up in business for yourself, you come up against taxation in several different ways. You may pay:

- income tax on your individual earnings, or on your profits, if you are a sole trader or partnership
- corporation tax on your profits if yours is a limited company, and if you are in the happy situation of making some profits
- Value Added Tax (VAT).

All taxes are liable to change at any time, not only with each year's budget. The monthly up-dating service of Croner's *Reference Book for*
▲ *the Self-employed and Smaller Business* (Croner House, 173 Kingston Road, New Malden, Surrey KT3 3SS, telephone: 01-942 8966) can be consulted at any time for the latest figures.

the first thing to do

As soon as you are ready to start trading, you should inform

- the inspector of taxes for your trading district
- your local Customs and Excise department (the VAT office), if there is any chance that you may want or need to be registered
- your local Department of Health and Social Security, about National Insurance.

Look up the local offices in your telephone directory; among the useful explanatory publications which they will send you, on request, are: *Starting in business* issued by the Board of Inland Revenue (IR.28) which includes a list of relevant leaflets, one on *Corporation Tax* (IR.18), also issued by the Board of Inland Revenue; *Value Added Tax general guide* (notice number 700) and *Value Added Tax scope and coverage* (notice number 701), and a leaflet entitled *Should I be registered for VAT?*, all issued by HM Customs and Excise.

income tax: directors of companies

If yours is a limited company, you, as one of its full-time directors, are an employee: you therefore pay income tax on your salary and on any bonus under the PAYE system, like any other employee. At the start of each trading year, you determine what your annual salary is to be, and you pay it to yourself monthly or weekly. Each time, you deduct income tax, according to instructions provided by Inland Revenue, to whom you send the deducted amounts. (In practice, this may be done not every week or month but, with the Inland Revenue's agreement, once a year.)

If, at the end of the trading year, the company accounts show a profit, you have the option of taking some or all of this profit as additional salary or bonus, and deducting tax from it. If there is another director with more than a nominal holding, the additional money would, of course, be distributed in proportion.

Whatever part of the profits is not taken in salary, is liable for (or, in Inland Revenue jargon, 'charged to') corporation tax. It is for you, in consultation with your accountant, to decide whether it is to your advantage to pay more income tax or more corporation tax; no general ruling is possible.

income tax: sole traders and partnerships

If you are a sole trader, or a partnership, there is no decision to be made: the whole of your business profits are treated as sole trader's or partner's income and taxed accordingly (under Schedule D); corporation tax does not apply.

choosing your accounting year

A firm's accounts are made up annually. This does not apply to the first trading period, which may be shorter than a year, or, for a sole trader or partnership, longer. But it is usual to call the day of the year on which you first close your books, your annual accounting date, and to go on using this day as the end of the trading year for as long as the firm continues in business.

It is for you to decide which day is to be your year's end. You may make it coincide with the end of the tax (financial) year, i.e. April 5th; or with the end of the calendar year. The Board of Inland Revenue suggests that if yours is a seasonal business, you should arrange to end your year in a slack period; your accountant may suggest a date soon after April 5th because, as will be explained later, this gives you the longest period for paying your taxes.

presenting accounts for inspection

The inspector of taxes requires to see the firm's trading account and profit and loss account, and sometimes the balance sheet (depending on the business concerned). He can ask for complete records of the whole of the firm's payments and receipts (including what has been drawn for private expenditure), supported by invoices, receipts, bank records and statements, paid cheques and cheque stubs.

It is best if the accounts are professionally drawn up by an accountant. Not only does he know the accepted way of presenting them, but he is able to make computations of allowances and adjustments which determine, after consultation with the Tax Inspector, what proportion of the profits is taxable. It is in your interest to make sure that all allowances are correctly claimed; this is a complex matter, best entrusted to an expert.

capital allowances

Capital expenditure is money spent on plant, buildings, machinery, vehicles, and anything else that has an enduring benefit for the business and does not need to be renewed every year. It is not, in itself, tax deductible, but allowances are given for the expenditure. In the case of a sole trader, these are set off against income for tax purposes. Capital expenditure incurred on such items prior to the setting up of the business, and capital expenditure in the first year, will qualify for allowances. If the allowances are not fully utilised, they may be carried forward to another year.

At present, a capital allowance of 100 per cent is given on plant machinery, office furniture and equipments, some motor vehicles and industrial buildings such as a small workshop (under 2,500 sq ft), in the 'first year', that is the year in which the capital expenditure is incurred. On other industrial buildings, the 'first year' allowance is 75 per cent, with the remaining 25 per cent being spread over 6 years.

Capital allowances are also granted on purchases of secondhand capital equipment, and the 100 per cent allowance is given on the cash price of capital items bought by hire-purchase. But in the case of leased equipment, the capital allowance goes to the lessor (generally a finance company) not you, the lessee.

stock relief

This is an adjustment intended to compensate the trader for the burden of maintaining stocks in a period of inflation.

When prices go up significantly during the year, the closing value of your stock will be shown as greater than the opening value, and this artificial increase is not deducted in arriving at your taxable profits (in fact, of course, you will be worse off since your stock will be costing more to replace). Stock relief is intended to compensate for this.

For each period of account, the relief is calculated as a percentage of the stock value at the end of the previous period, as measured by growth in an 'all-stocks' index. The first £2,000 of opening stock does not, however, qualify for relief.

In the past, the relief could be clawed back if stock values fell; now this can happen only if the firm's trade dwindles to almost nothing or ceases altogether.

deductible expenses

A portion of those expenses which are incurred wholly in the course of conducting the business can be set off against tax. Some of these are:
- wages of wife employed in the business (but they must be included in the husband's tax return as wife's income)
- expenses of business travel (but not of going to and from home to the main place of work unless a business call is made en route)
- interest on business loans
- interest charges on hire-purchase of capital equipment
- hire or leasing of equipment
- insurance premiums
- bad debts

– entertainment for overseas customers
– subscriptions to trade and professional associations
– cost of self-employed retirement annuity.

If your house or telephone are used partly for your business, you may claim against tax a proportion of the expenses (rent, rates, telephone rental, light, heating and so on). But if you claim half the rates against tax and for the period of your business only half the house is residential, and the other half is commercial, when you sell up to move, there is a potential Capital Gains Tax liability on the appreciation in value during that time: half the amount of the increase in value.

In the case of a car, some proportion of its cost (corresponding to the proportion of business use), may be claimed as capital allowance, and a similar proportion of the running costs may be claimed as a deductible business expense. You must, therefore, keep a record of the business mileage and the total mileage.

tax-deductible losses

Since a sole trader's (or partnership's) profits are taxed as income, losses may be set off against any income that the trader or his wife may receive from some other sources, in that year and the next.

Losses incurred in the first 4 years of trading may be set against wages or other income received in the 3 years before the trading started: a part of all the tax paid during that period will be refunded.

how business income tax is assessed

As a general rule, a business's tax assessment is based on profits which were earned in the trading year which ended in the previous tax year.

However, in the first 3 years of a new business, there are special rules for assessing business profits for tax. They are as follows:

First tax year (that is the year in which the business commenced): tax is assessed on profits from Day 1 of the first trading period to April 5th: if this trading period ends at some later date, a proportion is calculated on a time basis.

Second tax year: income tax is assessed on the profits of the first 12 months of trading; if the period exceeds 12 months, time apportionment applies.

Third tax year: income tax is assessed on the trading year ending in the previous tax year.

An example will make this clear. Tom started trading on May 5th, 1977, fixing May 4th as his year's end (accounting date). In his first trading year, his taxable profits were £900; in his second, they were £1,800; in his third, £2,400; in his fourth, £3,000.

tax year (6th–5th April)	assessment period from	assessment period to	taxable profits £
1977–1978	5.5.77	4.5.78	825 (11/12 of 900)
1978–1979	5.5.77	4.5.78	900
1979–1980	5.5.77	4.5.78	900
1980–1981	5.5.78	4.5.79	1,800
1981–1982	5.5.79	4.5.80	2,400
1982–1983	5.5.80	4.5.81	3,000

This shows that a new firm's profits in the first 3 years are assessed on the basis of the first year or eighteen months of trading, when profits are likely to be at their lowest. As they begin to increase, the basis of assessment shifts, until, in its fourth year, the assessment period follows the general rule for established businesses. Generally speaking, therefore, the first period's profits should be kept as low as possible for tax purposes because they are the basis for two or even three years' tax bills.

an optional basis of assessment

The trader has the choice of being assessed, in his second and third year of trading (not just one of these), on the actual profits made in those years, and not on the first trading period. Obviously, this option will be to his advantage only if his profits in the second and third years are lower than his first.

when tax is payable

Income tax is payable in two instalments, due on 1st January and 1st July. It is when you come to pay it that the importance of a good accounting date becomes apparent. Tom's trading period ends one month after the end of the tax year, which means that he will not be assessed for tax till nearly a year after his annual accounts are made up, and will not have to pay the tax till the following January and July. In fact, by choosing the right accounting date, you can obtain more than 2 years' grace from Inland Revenue.

changes to sole traders and partnerships

If a sole trader decides to take a partner, or a partnership takes an additional partner or partners or loses one or more, then for income tax purposes the business is usually deemed to have stopped trading when the old arrangement ended, and to have started trading again when the new arrangement started. However, this need not happen for tax purposes if all parties to both arrangements request the tax inspector, within 2 years of the change, to treat the trading as continuing.

corporation tax: limited companies

Most of what has been said about income tax on business profits (also known as Schedule D income tax) applies to the payment of corporation tax. This section will concentrate on differences between the two.

Corporation tax is the tax which companies pay on their profits. There are two different rates: the full rate of 52 per cent, and the reduced 'small company rate' of 40 per cent.

A small company is defined as one whose annual profits are £90,000 or less: up to this amount, the lower rate of 40 per cent is charged. As profits go above this, the relief for small companies is gradually reduced, until, at £225,000, the full rate of 52 per cent is paid.

how not to pay corporation tax

One material difference between a sole trader and a company lies in the fact that the salaries paid to company directors are a business cost, like any other salaries, and so are deducted in calculating profits. As the directors' remuneration need not be fixed until the results of the year's trading are known, it may be advantageous to a small company to pay out all its trading surplus as directors' salaries, on which they pay individual income tax. (For the remuneration to qualify as a deduction, however, the company must be able to show that it was paid or was made available 'wholly and exclusively for the purpose of the trade'.) Any part of the surplus that is not paid out is known as 'retained profit' and taxed at the corporation tax rate.

Your accountant will advise you how to apportion your profits between salaries and retained profit to your best advantage. He will also be needed for drawing up the accounts because, although corporation tax returns are not particularly complicated, the Companies Act demands more advanced and complex accounting from a company than is the case for a sole trader, and the company's accounts must be audited. So, professional help will certainly be needed.

capital allowances: limited company

These are the same for companies as for sole traders and partnerships, but cannot be set off against the directors' income from other sources: they apply only to the company's income. So if, for example, you were made redundant from a high-salary job and are likely to make a loss in the first year, be a sole trader – possibly changing to being a limited company after you have benefited fully from the original status.

A trading loss in any one period which is not due to the 'first year' capital allowance, may be set off retrospectively, against the previous year's profit only; claims must be made within 2 years. Or else the loss may be carried forward to offset the profits of subsequent years; the period in which losses may be carried forward is indefinite, but the claims must be made within 6 years.

accounting period: limited company

The first trading period for a company may be between 6 and 18 months, by company law. For corporation tax purposes, if it exceeds 12 months, the apportionments occur for a period of no more than 12 months.

Corporation tax is due 9 months from the end of the accounting period, or 30 days after the tax inspector has issued his notice of assessment, whichever is the later.

value added tax (VAT)

This is a tax payable quarterly, not to the Inland Revenue but to HM Customs and Excise, on the supply of most goods and services in Great Britain. It consists of input and output tax.

The tax you pay on goods and services that you buy for your business is called *input tax*: the tax you charge your customers is called *output tax*. At present, both are 15 per cent.

This is how it works: Bill buys raw materials for £230, inclusive of 15 per cent VAT; £30 is his input tax. He uses the materials to manufacture products selling for £450, exclusive of 15 per cent VAT. So the selling price would amount to £517.50 of which £67.50 is his output tax. He deducts the input tax from it, and remits the balance (£37.50) to Customs and Excise. If his input tax had been greater than his output tax, he would have been refunded the difference.

At present there are 3 categories of goods and services:

(1) *exempt:* on which no VAT is payable under any circumstances (for example, insurance, doctors' services)
(2) *zero-rated:* on which, in theory, tax could be payable but, in practice, none is (for example, exported goods, food in shops, books)
(3) *standard-rated:* on which VAT at 15 per cent is charged. The figure is liable to change at the government's decision.

The difference between (1) and (2) may seem trivial, but is actually important. You cannot claim refunds of input tax unless you are collecting output tax, if only notionally. If you dealt only in exempt supplies, you would not be a 'taxable person', and could not be registered for VAT. This would mean that you could not recover any of the input tax you paid on your supplies, such as telephone charges and stationery, any more than a private person can.

However, this is not the case if you deal only in zero-rated supplies (for example, if you are an exporter). You can claim refunds of your input tax – unless you exercise a zero-rated option of trader's exemption from VAT, in which case you lose these refunds.

registering for VAT

There are two kinds of registration: compulsory and voluntary.

compulsory registration

You must register for VAT if your taxable turnover is likely to exceed £17,000 in the year in which you start trading; or if you have already started trading, and at the end of the first quarter your taxable turnover is more than £5,000.

Trade in zero-rated supplies counts towards your turnover, but not trade in exempt supplies.

If you buy a going concern from a VAT-registered trader, you must be registered too – and may be allowed to go on using the same VAT registration number. (If you decide VAT registration is not to your advantage, perhaps if you intend to run the business on a smaller scale, you can apply for deregistration).

To register, contact your local VAT office, at Customs and Excise, who will send you forms to fill up. Once you have done this, you must immediately start charging your customers VAT and keeping records, without waiting to be allotted a registration number: because you yourself will be charged VAT from the moment you become liable for registration. So it is best not to get into arrears, which you may find it difficult to recover from your customers in retrospect. And it is worth setting up a system from the very beginning because it is hard to do 12 months' books in arrears.

You must keep records of all transactions. The Vatman's powers are sweeping: do not make guesses. Keep for inspection all invoices you receive which show payment of VAT. You have to make quarterly returns showing your input and output tax, and to submit to having your VAT records inspected at intervals.

voluntary registration

With a turnover under £17,000 a year, you may still apply for registration if you are able to convince Customs and Excise that this is necessary for the health of your business.

Some of the advantages of registration are:
– You can claim back all your input tax (for instance, on equipment you have to buy when setting up). This is especially advantageous if your goods or services are zero-rated.
– If you start trading unregistered and your turnover grows to the point where you have to register, the addition of VAT will increase all your prices: this will dismay your customers, if they are consumers and not registered traders, and so cannot claim back the increase.
– VAT can ease your cash flow difficulties. If you arrange to make major purchases just before you are due to make out a return, your input VAT will be refunded shortly after you get the invoice, even though you may be receiving 3 months' credit from your suppliers. (But this scheme will work against you if you yourself give credit to customers: you will have to pay your output VAT months before you yourself get paid.)

Some of the disadvantages of registration are:
– The record-keeping and accounting demanded by VAT are an addition to your labours which you may not welcome if you employ a small office staff, or none. Matters become still more complicated if you deal in a variety of goods, some standard-rated and others zero-rated, for example stationery and books.
– If you are an exporter, you must be able to prove (by means of the relevant shipping documents) that your goods were, in fact, sold abroad. If some of your trade is in export and some is home trade, you will have the complication of selling goods differently rated.

How to be an employer

Yes, there is such a thing as a one-man business, particularly if what is being offered is a service or a consultancy. A plumber or electrician, for instance, needs only a telephone-answering machine to record customers' calls: he calls them back in the evenings, and does his book-keeping on sundays.

Many small firms start up with no other staff than the entrepreneur himself and his family, or a partner. But unless the family is large and willing, the firm will soon be needing some other employees, if it is to achieve progress.

In fact, a manufacturing business is likely to need employees from the start. It may only be a case of a couple of part-timers, or outworkers, or one trained secretary; even so, the businessman immediately becomes an employer, and should find out how to go about it.

finding and recruiting staff

When you have decided to take on employees, start by defining exactly what their duties are to be and what experience, skills and qualities are required to do the job. Avoid the temptation to ask for experience and qualifications greater than are necessary. This will make it easier for you to find the right person and easier, also, for any applicant to decide whether the job is the right one for him or her. A good working relationship is much more likely to develop if both you and your workers are well suited to each other.

Ways of finding suitable employees include the public employment service (jobcentre or careers office, both listed in the telephone directory), employment agencies (which charge the employer a fee) personal recommendation or advertisements in your local or national or trade press or local radio stations.

If you have a shop or factory with an entrance on the main road, place an advertisment where it can be seen by passers-by. Or advertise for new workers by placing cards in local shops. This is cheap and generally produces a good response. Specify exactly what is wanted – and if you are willing to train new staff, make this clear.

It is sometimes easier and more economical to employ more casual workers than full-time staff, particularly when employing young mothers who are keen to get jobs which can be done partly at home or with flexible hours, perhaps not coming into work during school holidays.

It can be a bad mistake to employ aquaintances; this can prove embarrassing if they are no good. Also, do not try to recruit staff when you already have large orders and are very busy. This would be inefficient because it does not allow time for training.

Remember that any advertisement, wherever it is placed, must not exclude anyone on grounds of race or sex except in a very few closely defined cases.

Local jobcentres provide a fast, free recruitment service for all types of jobs, and jobcentre staff can advise on selection and can provide general information on employment legislation.

You may decide to employ young people and train them yourself: the government offers some financial incentives to firms willing to help reduce unemployment among school leavers. Consult your local careers service office or jobcentre about this and for advice on training.

If you are looking for a worker with a particular skill which is in short supply locally, your local jobcentre can give a wide circulation to the vacancy, to attract workers from other areas.

A worker with a particular skill may be already employed elsewhere and you may need to offer him terms that are in some way an improvement on what he is getting or can get in his present job, in order to attract him away. If he is at present employed locally, make sure his contract of employment does not prohibit him from leaving to take up a similar job within, say, five miles of his existing place of employment, otherwise he and you could end up with a costly court case.

If you ask for references, be sure to take them up, preferably by telephone. The previous employer will probably prove more frank in speaking to you in confidence, than in writing. A particularly glowing reference always provokes the suspicion that the previous employers are anxious to part with its subject.

avoiding disputes

In addition to the relevant government agencies, the independent Advisory, Conciliation and Arbitration Service (ACAS) can be consulted on matters relating to employment. Though this organisation is mostly known to the public as conciliator in industrial disputes, the chief part of its work is preventive and consists of advising both sides of industry on how to find their way through the complications of employment legislation.

▲ The ACAS head office address is: 11 St. James's Square, London SW1Y 4LA (telephone: 01-214 6000) and there are ten regional offices. ACAS has published a series of (free) advisory booklets on such topics as recruitment and selection, induction of new employees, job evaluation, and other aspects of employment.

Some small businessmen are unreasonably frightened of employing anyone – so much so, that they stunt their firm's growth by not taking on the necessary staff. But really, there is nothing to fear but fear itself.

The acrimonious industrial disputes featured in the newspapers and on TV seldom affect the small businesses, which have, as a rule, good industrial relations. This may be because workers and 'boss' work in close contact with each other and have a common interest in making the firm do well. This does not mean, of course, that as a small employer you are exempt from the laws enacted to protect the employee. On the contrary, if you want to promote harmony, you will attend to them scrupulously: the most important ones are those concerned with hiring, firing and working conditions.

statement of the terms of employment

Every employee who works for you full-time (or part-time for more than 16 hours a week), must by law be provided, within 13 weeks of starting work, with a written statement setting out the conditions and terms on which he is employed. (This is sometimes called a 'contract of employment' though that is not strictly correct: the contract was formed earlier, when you made someone a firm offer of a job and it was firmly accepted. This is legally enforceable as soon as an employee starts work.)

The written statement must contain information on at least these points:

- name of the employer and employee
- whether employment with a previous employer counts as part of continuous period of employment
- date of starting employment
- title or description of employee's job
- rates of pay (including overtime, if any) and how they are calculated
- times when payment is made (weekly or monthly)
- hours of work (regular and overtime, if applicable)
- holidays and holiday pay
- sick pay arrangements
- pension scheme arrangements and whether a contracting-out certificate under the Social Security Pensions Act 1975 is in force
- length of notice required from employer and from employee
- rules relating to disciplinary procedures, such as warnings and dismissal, and procedure for taking up grievances.

If any of these points do not apply, for instance if there are no pension arrangements, the document must say so explicitly. Look at some actual statements of terms before drafting your own. Further information and an example of a written statement can be found in the Department of Employment's booklet *Written statement of main terms and conditions of employment* which is available free from jobcentres, employment offices and unemployment benefit offices.

It is the practice of many employers to confirm an oral offer of job by a letter, setting out the conditions and terms. If all these above points are covered, such a letter will do in place of a written statement; if they are not, a written statement will still be necessary.

Part-time workers employed for less than 16 hours and more than 8 hours a week are also entitled to a written statement of employment, but only after they have worked for you for 5 years – but, of course, you do not have to wait till then.

The terms set out in the statement cannot be altered without the consent of both parties. If you transfer the employee to another kind of work or promote him, he no longer has the same job and may need a new written statement.

paying wages and salaries

To a certain extent, a new business sets its own rates of pay, depending on how much it expects to be able to afford. However, in some trades and industries there is a minimum legal wage laid down by a wages council, so you would do well to check whether your business comes under such a ruling. If it does, and you pay your workers less than the minimum, you risk prosecution. Wages councils may also make legally binding regulations about holidays and sick pay: to find out whether any of these regulations apply to you, consult the Department of
▲ Employment Wages Inspectorate, Caxton House, Tothill Street, London SW1H 9NF.

Another factor affecting wage levels may be an agreement between the employers' federation of your trade and the appropriate trade unions which may be binding on you. If there are similar businesses in the area, it is wise to find out what they are paying, and if it is related to a union rate.

Men and women doing the same or broadly similar work are, of course, entitled to the same rates of pay.

With each wage payment, you must give each employee a wage slip showing his gross pay, itemised deductions (such as income tax, National Insurance contributions, union dues) and the net pay. Keep a copy for your own records, and if you pay wages in cash, get your copy signed by the employee, as a receipt. You must also keep a wages book: your accountant will tell you how to set one up, and may even agree, for a fee, to look after your payroll until you are sufficiently organised to take care of it yourself.

some workers' rights

A pregnant employee has the right to time off without loss of pay for visits to antenatal clinics. Where an employee is leaving work to have a baby and has worked for you for at least 2 years (or five years if she works between 8 and 16 hours a week) up to the eleventh week before her confinement (and fulfils certain other qualifying conditions), you must give her at least 90 per cent of her normal pay, less flat-rate maternity allowance whether or not she receives this, for the first 6 weeks of her absence – whether or not she is coming back for you. You can claim a full rebate for this from the Maternity Pay Fund (administered by the Department of Employment's redundancy payments offices) provided you were actually liable to pay maternity pay to the employee.

If your employee fulfils the qualifying conditions, she is entitled to come back to work for you in her former job (or a suitable alternative where it is not reasonably practical for you to offer her the former job) at any time up to the end of the 29th week after the birth of the child. But she must tell you this (in writing at least 21 days before her absence begins) and must produce a certificate of expected confinement, if you want to see it. Not earlier than 49 days after the expected confinement, you may write to ask her if she still intends to return and she must reply within 14 days and must let you know the date on which she wants to return at least 21 days in advance.

From April 1983, the statutory sick pay scheme will mean that an employer has to pay employees during the first 8 weeks of sickness to enable the employer to get a rebate from the government (similar to that under the maternity pay scheme).

dismissing an employee

Employment enjoys so much legal protection that it is essential for every employer to know exactly when and in what circumstances he may dismiss an employee.

Going about it the wrong way can lead to a complaint of unfair dismissal to an industrial tribunal, and if this body finds against you, it has the power to order re-employment of, or an award of compensation to, the employee. Such an award can be crippling to a small business; what is more, you will in most cases have to pay the costs of defending yourself, win or lose.

You cannot just sack an employee on the spot, however provoked you may be. An employee who has worked for you for four weeks or more is entitled to a week's notice or a week's salary in lieu of notice. After two years, he must have one week's notice for each year of working for you, up to a maximum of 12 weeks. Every employee working 16 hours or more a week, who has been employed for six months of more, is entitled to a written statement of the reason why he is being dismissed, if he asks for one. In a firm employing fewer than 20 people, a statement of reason for dismissal need only be given to someone who has been employed there for two years or more.

Except in the case of wholly intolerable misconduct, it is unwise to dismiss anyone for a first offence. Put yourself in the right by discussing the matter with the employee and listening to what he has to say. An employer must make proper investigations into any suspicion of misconduct and allow his employee to state his side of the case, and bring along someone to represent him.

It is important to send him a written warning, explaining exactly what fault you find with his work and/or conduct, and demanding that he mend his ways – or risk dismissal.

If there is no improvement, send a second warning, and, if necessary, a third, keeping copies of all of them; after which you are fairly safe in giving notice without the risk of a complaint of unfair dismissal succeeding against you provided that you can prove the facts leading to the dismissal.

Every dismissed employee who has been continuously employed for one year – or two years, in the case of a firm employing 20 or fewer people – may bring a complaint of unfair dismissal to an industrial tribunal. The latter will take account of the firm's size and resources when deciding whether a dismissal was fair or not, and whether to direct re-employment. For instance, if the worker has proved not up to the physical demands of the job, a small firm may not have another job to offer him, and may therefore dismiss him.

Further information can be found in the Department of Employment booklet *The law on unfair dismissal: guide for small firms,* available free from jobcentres, employment offices, unemployment benefit offices or the Department of Industry's Small Firms Centres. The Consumer Publication *Getting a new job* deals, amongst other things, with industrial tribunals, unfair dismissal, and redundancy. A two-day course on basic employment law is amongst the courses organised by
▲ The Industrial Society, Peter Runge House, 3 Carlton House Terrace, London SW1Y 5DG (telephone: 01-839 4300). Other of their courses range from 'Achieving people's commitment at work' to 'Understanding financial information'.

making employees redundant

Employees may have to be made redundant when a firm is not doing enough business to justify their employment. A redundancy dismissal can be unfair on the basis of improper selection, lack of consultation and lack of notice. It should certainly not be motivated by personal reasons. A worker who thinks you are making him redundant just to get rid of him can challenge your decision before an industrial tribunal.

Anyone whom you have employed continuously for two years is entitled to redundancy pay, the amount of which will depend on the person's rate of pay and length of employment. Some of this money (at present 41 per cent) will be refunded by the Department of Employment, whose advice you should seek if you have to cope with redundancies.

In fact, there is an obligation on the employer to inform his local Department of Employment if he is going to make anyone redundant, otherwise he will lose his rebate of 41 per cent. You will find the address of your local office in the telephone directory.

One important point to be aware of if you take over a going concern, is that workers' employment is deemed in law to be continuing. So if you decide to replace some of them, you may find yourself with a good deal of compensation to pay, even though you did not hire these people, and they have not worked for you very long. This is one of the dangers of taking over a going concern, so before you do so, ask for a roll of employees, showing their length of continuous employment there, so that you can assess the amount of possible redundancy pay.

health and safety of employees

The responsibilities concerning the health, safety and welfare of people at work are defined in broad terms by the Health and Safety at Work etc Act 1974. It places important general duties on all people at work – employers, employees and the self-employed, manufacturers, suppliers, designers and importers of materials used at work, and people in control of premises. More detailed and specific requirements for particular kinds of work are laid down by other legislation, such as the Offices Shops and Railways Premises Act 1963 which specifies what must be provided in the way of washrooms, lavatories, heat, ventilation and light, somewhere to sit, and so on. The Factories Act 1961 and other statutes and regulations apply to many different work activities.

The requirements to protect health and safety and provide welfare, which must be complied with by each kind of small business, vary considerably depending on the type of work being carried on. You will need to find out, preferably at an early stage, how your business will be affected and what facilities and safeguards you must provide in matters such as, for instance, machinery guards, protective clothing, storage and handling of dangerous substances.

If in doubt, consult the appropriate enforcing authority – who will come to inspect your premises. Generally, the enforcing authority is the local authority for most shops, offices, hotel and catering activities. For other businesses, it is the Health and Safety Executive.

Addresses of local authority enforcement offices can be obtained from district council offices or, in case of difficulty, from the local authority liason officer in the nearest Health and Safety area office. There are some 20 Health and Safety area offices; the general enquiry point for them is the Health and Safety Executive, Baynards House, 1 Chepstow Place, London W2 4TF (telephone: 01-229 3456).

The Health and Safety Executive publishes a range of explanatory and guidence material; some publications are available free of charge from HSE offices; the booklet *A guide to the HSW Act* (HS(R)6), obtainable from HMSO or booksellers, costs £2.75.

All accidents at work must be recorded and all serious ones, which lead to having 3 or more days off or at least one day in hospital, must be reported on a special form to the local Health and Safety Executive. Near-miss accidents must also be reported. Every place of work should have a well-equipped first aid box, the contents of which are specified, and the employees should know where it is kept and there should be someone trained to use it.

agent for the government

You are the channel by which your employees' PAYE income tax is transmitted to the Board of Inland Revenue, as well as their National Insurance contributions (and yours, too).

coping with PAYE

If you employ anyone in your business in return for wages, even members of your own family, you are responsible for deducting their income tax at source and sending it to the Inland Revenue. This you do every month, even if you pay wages weekly and therefore make the deductions every week.

An employee who has previously been employed and paid tax should bring you his form P 45 which has on it his code number and total pay and total tax to date in the financial year. A new employee who has not paid PAYE tax before, must be given form P 46 which you can get from the Inland Revenue office, and an emergency code number.

When you tell the tax inspector that you will be an employer, he will send you two sets of printed tables, *Free pay table A*, and *PAYE taxable pay tables B–D*. By looking up each code number in the tables, you will know how much tax to deduct each week or month. You enter the amount, the gross salary and other details on each employee's deductions working sheet, which has a space for each week of the tax year.

At the end of the tax year, all the information concerning each employee's wages, income tax and National Insurance contributions must be entered on a triplicate form (P 14), two copies of which are sent to the Collector of Taxes who passes one of them on to the Department of Health and Social Security; the third (Certificate P 60) goes to the employee.

National Insurance

As an employer, you are also responsible for collecting all your employees' National Insurance contributions every week or month, together with their income tax, and sending them on to Inland Revenue (not the DHSS) together with yours, the employer's contributions.

Arrangements exist for employees to contract out of part of their contributions where a firm has an occupational pension scheme, but this is unlikely to concern you at this stage.

You will be concerned with 3 kinds of contributions, as listed:

National Insurance contributions (as from August 1982)

Type of contribution	Category of insured person	Basis of contribution	Earnings limits lower	upper	Amount paid
Class 1	employed earners	earnings-related	£29.50 a week	£220 a week	8.75% employee 12.02% employer
Class 2	self-employed	flat rate	——	——	£3.75 a week
Class 4	self-employed	earnings-related	£3,450 annual profits	£11,000	6% of amount by which profits exceed lower limit, up to £453 p.a.

class 1 contributions

These are due from each of your employees who is over sixteen and below the minimum pension age (65 for a man, 60 for a woman) whose earnings reach the lower earning limit. For each of them, you must pay the employer's share. (Contributions are not due from employees over pension age, but you must continue to pay the employer's share.) Obviously the lower earnings limit figure (at the present, £29.50) is one to bear in mind when employing part-time staff. If you go over this limit, both the employee and you have to pay National Insurance contributions. You would need to increase the employee's pay by £4 for him to get an increase of 21p in take-home pay after National Insurance contributions and tax have been deducted.

If yours is a limited company, you as an individual pay an employee's share, and the company pays the employer's contribution – although in effect, in a small company you would be paying both the sums.

class 2 contributions

You pay these if you are a sole trader or a partner, and there are some benefits from which you are excluded, notably unemployment benefit.

You can claim exemption from class 2 payments if you are able to show that your net earnings from self-employment in a tax year are expected to be below a certain sum (£1,600 in 1982/3). You must apply to the DHSS for an exemption certificate in advance. The certificate cannot normally be back-calculated, and any contributions already paid cannot be refunded.

If you start your business in your spare time while continuing to work for an employer, you must pay both class 1 and class 2 contributions. There is, however, an upper limit, and anything you pay over this amount in a tax year will be refunded to you. (In 1982/3 the limit is £1,022.11)

There are several ways of paying. You can buy a stamp every week at a post office, and stick it on a contribution card which your local DHSS office will send you; or you can arrange to pay by direct debit, through your bank or National Girobank.

class 4 contributions

These are payable by class 2 payers whose taxable profits exceed a certain sum; there is an upper limit on the amount payable.

Class 4 contributions are assessed together with income tax by the Inland Revenue. If you expect your contributions to go over the set limits in any year, you can apply to defer the payment till your earnings have been assessed for tax. It is worth remembering that you can claim capital allowances, stock relief and trading losses against your class 4 liabilities, just as you can against income tax.

For fuller information about National Insurance, go directly to the source, the DHSS; the following leaflets, updated every year, should be consulted:

NI 40   National Insurance Guide for Employees
NP 15   Employer's Guide to National Insurance Contributions
NI 208   National Insurance Contribution Rates
NI 41   National Insurance Guide for the Self-employed
NP 28   More Than One Job? (Class 1 Contributions)
NP 18   Class 4 NI Contributions
NP 27A People with small earnings from self-employment.

Insurance for the small business

When you are just starting up in business and every penny counts, having to pay insurance premiums can seem to be an uncalled-for imposition. But you would see this in a different light if the occasion arose to put in a claim. Then you might start to worry whether you had taken enough insurance to cover all the losses you had suffered.

Insurance is best thought of as the price of peace of mind. Calamities will happen, as everyone knows. Make sure, if you take out insurance, that the cover is adequate – otherwise, you might as well not bother.

Almost every aspect of trading can create a need for some kind of insurance. For most kinds you can find cover, but sometimes the premium may be high.

The premiums paid for any business insurance are deductible expenses which can be set off against tax.

employer's liability insurance

The law requires that everyone on your payroll (except for members of your family and domestic servants), must be covered by this insurance, and that a current certificate of insurance be displayed at the place of work.

The employer's liability insurance covers you for claims that might arise because an employee suffered physical injury or illness in the course of, or resulting from, his employment. This could be anything from a twisted ankle after falling down stairs to losing a limb. It would be necessary for the employee suing you for damages to show that the injury or illness arose not from his own inadvertence, but out of your negligence or that of another employee.

You would be wise to include employed members of the family in the insurance cover, even though you do not need to. Close relationship does not preclude a claim for damages, and if one of your nearest and dearest were to suffer, you would be glad to have them compensated by the insurance company.

Most insurance companies will quote you rates for this type of insurance. The premiums are related to the size of your payroll and will also depend on the risks attached to the jobs. If your employees do office work only, it is likely to cost less than if they work with machinery or shift heavy loads.

▲ The Health & Safety Executive, 1 Chepstow Place, London W2 4TF (telephone: 01-229 3456) has published a small brochure *Short Guide to the Employer's Liability (Compulsory Insurance) Act 1969*, which is available free on request.

material damage insurance

You would be foolhardy not to insure for the various disasters that could mean the rapid end of your business, such as burglary, fire, flood, subsidence, malicious damage, explosion, to name but a few. Some of the features of a business that should be covered are

– the business premises (including site clearance and rebuilding costs)
– their contents (including fixtures and fittings, industrial plant, tools and other equipment)
– the stock (including supplies not yet used and goods that have been allocated to customers, even if the customer has not yet paid for them)
– goods in transit (on the way to the customer, or to a sub-contractor, or to the docks for shipment; in your own or someone else's vehicles; sent by post)
– goods on a sub-contractor's premises.

You could take out a separate policy for each kind of risk, but it would be more efficient to have a single material damage insurance policy covering them all.

Many trade associations arrange (or act as agents for) special insurance policies tailored for the needs of the particular trade.

The insurance should be revised and updated at regular intervals, otherwise you might find a huge discrepancy between the amount you are covered for and what your loss actually amounts to.

consequential loss insurance

This is a corollary to material damage insurance: it covers further losses which would arise if your business were to come to a standstill following a disaster that is covered by the insurance. Should your premises burn down, for instance, you would not only need to rebuild and re-equip but would also have to pay your wage bill and some overhead costs while no money is coming in. You may have lost all your stock and your office records and files, and by the time you are back in business, your customers may have gone elsewhere.

Consequential loss insurance should cover all these situations, loss of profit, and your overhead costs for a limited period (known as the indemnity period). Usually this is not less than 12 months; you may be able to negotiate a longer period, and the particular features of your business may need other special terms.

public liability insurance

Apart from the statutory insurance for liability to employees, there is insurance to cover you for claims by members of the public who have been injured as a result of your (or one of your employees') activities at work: for example, a brick dropped from a scaffolding on a passer's-by head.

product liability insurance

This covers you for claims arising out of faults in something you or you employees have manufactured or serviced – if your folding chair collapses under a purchaser, say, or the washing machine you have repaired gives a severe electrical shock.

insurance for car and driver

Third-party insurance is, of course, compulsory on all the firm's vehicles; and you should insure at the same time for theft and accidents, etc. If your vehicles are going to be driven by various persons, make sure yours is an all-drivers policy.

If your work involves a great deal of driving, you would be wise to insure for loss of your driving licence, which could otherwise mean the loss of your livelihood. The insurance company cannot restore your licence, but it can supply the means to hire a chauffeur.

insurance if money is lost

A policy of this sort will cover you for loss of money (including cheques and postal orders) from your office, your till, from your house, or in transit – for instance, you could be robbed while taking it to the bank. Insurance can also be taken out to compensate an employee who is injured while being robbed of money.

Firms who hold clients' money, such as travel agents or insurance agents, need an insurance bond to protect it against loss if the business fails. Bonding is compulsory for some types of agency.

personal insurance

You might consider private health insurance. One reason would be that if you were confined to bed in hospital, you would have a room to yourself, and a telephone, and could keep in touch with your business to an extent impossible in a public ward. You could have some control over the timing of a non-urgent operation, so that it coincided with a slack business period, for example.

If you start a business alone, without a partner, an illness or accident which takes you out of circulation for any length of time could be damaging – or fatal – to your prospects. You can take out a policy to cover these contingencies.

There is also a 'key person' insurance under which a limited company, a partnership or sole proprietor can obtain cover for loss of profit suffered as the consequence of the death of the proprietor, managing director, partner or senior employee. Any claim would be met either by a single lump sum or a number of annual instalments for some years following the death of the key person.

It is possible to get insurance to cover the cost of replacement personnel if a key person is called for jury service.

In a partnership, it is possible to get insurance for the eventuality of having to buy the partner's share in the business from his inheritors, in the event of the partner's death.

other insurance

There is hardly a calamity for which you cannot insure your business or yourself. For instance, if you have a shop, you might enquire about a plate glass insurance policy, which would provide such facilities as having your broken window and/or door boarded up, speedy replacement of the glass, compensation for damage or injury by shattered glass, consequential loss of profits.

You can insure to cover being robbed or defrauded by your employees; you can even insure in case you are made to pay compensation by an industrial tribunal.

▲ By becoming a member of the National Federation of Self-Employed and Small Businesses, 45 Russell Square, London WC1 (telephone: 01-636 3828), you are automatically entitled to insurance, with a cover of up to £10,000, for the expenses of VAT tribunal cases; Health and Safety at Work Act prosecutions; 90 per cent of any awards made by industrial tribunals; private and business motoring prosecutions.

If any other risk occurs to you, it is worth while finding out if any insurers will cover you for it.

brokers

You can never insure against anything, only for the cash compensation for any loss that you may suffer as a result of a happening. Insurance is a major industry, complex and rather specialised, so there may be a case for getting the advice of an insurance broker specialising in commercial insurance, particularly if you need some unusual type of insurance or if you are faced with what seem excessively high premium demands.

▲ An insurance broker is an agent for the sale of insurance whose task it is to match his clients' requirements with the right insurance companies. His commission is paid by the insurers, based on the business he brings them. In finding a good insurance broker, personal recommendation is likely to be best; or you might get in touch with BIBA, the British Insurance Brokers Association, Fountain House, 130 Fenchurch Street, London EC3 MEJ (telephone: 01-623 9043) and ask for the names of some brokers willing to serve a small business, and make your choice from these.

Protecting your business idea

If your business project is based on an original idea or invention, you will naturally want to exploit it for your sole benefit for as long as possible.

There are various ways of protecting a business idea, which of them you choose depends on the nature of the idea and also on what you expect that your sole right to it will be worth. Protecting a business idea can be expensive, especially if the protection needs to be valid in several countries, so you must be sure that the resulting benefit will be worth the expense. There should be a sound commercial reason for seeking to establish a sole right.

Moreover, if this is infringed, your only redress lies in the courts of law, and going to law can be wasteful of time and money, whether you win or lose.

patents

A patent is the common way of establishing a legal claim to the ownership and sole exploitation of an invention. To be patentable, an invention must be new, must constitute an inventive advance – that is, something more than just an improvement on something already known or made – and must be capable of being used in industry or agriculture.

It is essential not to disclose its nature publicly before the patent application has been filed at the Patent Office. Once an idea has been made public, an application to patent it can be rejected on the grounds that it is no longer new.

'patent applied for'

To obtain a patent, the inventor files an application (current fee £10)
▲ with the Patent Office (25 Southampton Buildings, London WC2 1AY), together with a detailed description and/or specification of the invention. His priority claim begins with the moment the application is received at the Patent Office.

He now has 12 months to decide whether to pursue the application or let it lapse. If he also wants protection abroad, now is the time to seek it. A european patent can now be applied for, and gives protection in several countries simultaneously; other foreign patents, if required, should also be applied for during the 12-month period.

If the inventor elects to pursue his application, he pays a fee (currently £63) and files a claim and an abstract of the invention. The invention as defined in the claim is then searched by a patent examiner to see whether it is new and inventive. A report, which lists documents that might have a bearing on the application, is sent to the inventor. About 18 months from the date of filing, the application is published and any interested third parties, such as other inventors, can write to the Patent Office making observations on the patentability of the invention. Such letters might draw attention to documents which are considered to show that the invention is not totally new or does not involve 'inventiveness'. Third parties do not take part in the examination proceedings which follow, but the examiner does consider their observations.

Within 6 months of publication, the inventor must decide whether to enter the last stage. If he does, he must pay a fee (currently £75).

The application is now closely scrutinised to see whether it complies with all the requirements of the Patent Act, for instance, does it work? is the description adequate? is the invention novel and inventive? The examiner pursues any objections with the inventor, until he is satisfied.

The application is then granted and published in its finally agreed form. The grant is for 20 years from the date of filing, subject to the payment of annual renewal fees from the fifth year onwards.

After the grant, interested third parties can apply for revocation of the patent on various grounds, and the inventor can defend it.

how to go about it

An inventor can deal with the Patent Office direct, but it may be better to employ a patent agent to look after the inventor's interest. (Names can be obtained from the secretary, Chartered Institute of Patent ▲ Agents, Staple Inn, Holborn, London WC2 (telephone: 01-405 9450).

Pamphlets entitled *Applying for a Patent*, and *Instructions for the Preparation of Drawings in Patent Applications*, a list of fees and the various forms required are available, free, from the Patent Office.

trade marks

The function of a trade mark is to identify the product of the owner of the mark (generally the manufacturer). It does not necessarily have to be registered, provided the owner can establish the use and reputation of the mark. While registration of a trade mark is not mandatory in order to obtain protection for it at law, if the mark is currently registered under the Trade Mark Act 1938 it makes it much simpler for the owner to have recourse against any person infringing the mark or passing off his goods as those of the owner.

Trade marks may consist of a device (a picture or logo) and word or words, and signature, or some combination of these. A marked proposed for registration has to meet strict criteria in order to qualify: it must be distinctive, must not be deceptive, and must not be easily confused with other marks already registered in respect of similar kinds of goods. So, some trade marks proposed for registration are inherently unregistrable or have to be modified; others are unregistrable because a similar mark for similar sort of goods has already been registered.

applying for a trade mark

Application to register a trade mark has to be made to the registrar at the Patent Office who sees whether it complies with the provisions of the Trade Mark Act 1938. If it is considered acceptable, or will be acceptable after it has been modified, the mark is advertised in the Trade Marks Journal. If no objections are raised by any third parties within a set period, it is entered in the register for an initial period of 7 years. After this, the mark may be renewed for periods of 14 years at a time, with no upper time limit to the registration.

But a trade mark may be removed from the register if a claimant proves that it has been wrongly registered or that it has not been used or that it has lost its power to distinguish.

Each mark must relate to only one classification of goods. A list of the classifications can be obtained from the registrar. A pamphlet entitled *Applying for a Trade Mark*, which lists fees, and the necessary forms are available without charge from the Trade Marks Registry at the ▲ Patent Office. The telephone number of the Patent Office is 01-405 8721.

registered designs

Registering the design of some invention, or other object, is a method of protecting not the way in which it functions (which should be protected by a patent), but the way it looks: its appearance.

The designer applies to the Designs Registry at the Patent Office, furnishing a representation, or specimen, or photographs of the design. The design is examined to see whether it is new or original and complies with other requirements of the Registered Designs Act 1949. If it does, a certificate of registration is issued, which gives the proprietor the sole right to manufacture, sell or use in business, articles which look identical (or very similar) to the design submitted for registration. The fee depends on the nature of the article and design – from £10 to £72, at present. This protection lasts for 5 years in the first instance, and can be renewed for two further periods of 5 years.

The protection is intended to apply to industrial designs, that is, only the appearance of articles manufactured in quantities of more than 50. Its scope does not cover such features as shape or configurations that are strictly part of the function of the article. This means that the appearance of many mechanical components and articles whose shape is determined solely by the need to do the job, and not by its appeal to the eye, cannot be protected as a registered design. (Such articles may however be protected by copyright if an original drawing exists).

A pamphlet entitled *Protection of Industrial Designs*, which also lists fees, and the necessary forms are availabe free of charge from the Design Registry at the Patent Office.

copyright

The law of copyright forbids the unauthorised reproduction of an artist's or craftsman's work.

It was originally brought in to protect authors' rights in their written work, and was later extended to other media, such as films, records and the graphic arts. Engineering drawings are also protected. What is most important, copyright is infringed if such drawings are copied in three dimensions, that is, if they are reproduced in the form of objects.

No registration is required, but the author or draughtsman needs to be able to prove authorship: he should be able to show his original drawing and the rough drawings it was based on. All of these should have been signed, dated, and the signature witnessed; preferably they should be marked with the international copyright symbol, 'c' inside a circle, © accompanied by the year of first publication and the copyright owner's name.

Copyright protection lasts for the author's/designer's lifetime, and for 50 years after his death.

getting help

If you need to take out a patent or register a trade mark or a design, you will be well advised to seek the help of a patent agent, because the legislation relating to all of these is complex. Londoners can use the London Enterprise Agency's free innovations service for advice on protecting new ideas, and similar agencies may be able to offer help in other areas of the country.

If you want to thread your own way through the maze, the Patent Office building also houses the Science Reference Library (Holborn), which contains literature concerned with inventions, patents, trade marks, and so on, and which is open to the public.

Being a retailer

Every High Street is the same – every High Street is different: para-doxically, both statements are true. From town to town, the first impression is of sameness, with the familiar chain stores and multiples Boots, W.H. Smith, Sainsbury's and many others in various combi-nations in every shopping centre of any size. But if you look more closely, you will notice among the famous fascias many belonging to the smaller businesses, with just the one shop, or perhaps one or two branches. And in villages and suburban shopping parades the individual businesses will be in the majority; some old-established, others recently started, all determined to keep their end up.

These are not easy times for retail businesses: the shopkeepers are fighting the huge organisations for a share of the customers' dwindling spending power, and are using considerable ingenuity in doing so.

The multiples, with their enormous resources, vast floor space and the ability to command the whole output of a factory, have an undoubted advantage in cutting prices and offering a large variety of lines. The smaller shops that do not evolve and adapt to meet this challenger are fighting tanks with blowpipes.

Some practise guerrilla warfare, turning their small size to advantage in offering some kinds of service that are not worth the big organi-sations' while: opening very early or staying open very late; delivering to customers' houses; and various others. The small shop's strongest weapon is the element of service which is the one thing the giants cannot match. Many people prefer to spend their money where veg-etables and groceries will be delivered, a dress altered to fit exactly, do-it-yourself tools sold with some expert advice.

The small shop can sell goods in small quantities: one slice of ham, half a yard of elastic, six screws; in the big stores, such items are prepacked, giving the customer little control over quantity. Such a service is especially valuable to elderly people whose needs are modest, as are their means. Still, if a shop attracts all the pensioner trade, it should not complain.

The small shop can attract custom by being willing to gratify a few customers by ordering uncommon products especially. It also has a social value: people who feel lost in impersonal supermarkets appreciate the personal attention and friendliness of the individual shop-keepers, as well as the chance of chatting with neighbours.

Service means labour, and labour is expensive, even though it is, alas for many, no longer so scarce as it used to be. Consider ways of turning this melancholy situation to advantage, perhaps by employing school-leavers or taking on part-timers. You score if you can harness the whole family into a team, perhaps – if yours is a shop that is allowed to – opening seven days a week (usually only possible if the shop is staffed by the owner's family).

opening hours

The trading hours of shops are regulated by the Shops Act 1950, the gist of which is that shops may open at whatever time they like, but must close by 8 pm on weekdays, 9 pm on one week night (late shopping night), in many places the friday. Shops may open on sundays to sell a limited range of goods: newspapers, magazines, cigarettes, tobacco, sweets, milk, fresh vegetables, cooked food and various other items, usually of a perishable nature, or related to entertainment (guide books, postcards) or emergencies (medicines, surgical appliances).

Shops must close by 1 pm one day a week (not necessarily all on the same one) unless the majority of the shopkeepers in the district petition for this regulation to be relaxed. Some shops are exempt from the early closing rule: the criteria are roughly the same as for sunday opening.

There are relaxations for shops in holiday areas, which may stay open on some sundays to sell holiday goods (e.g., camera film, fishing rods). Some shops owned by Jews which close on saturdays, may open on sundays.

You will probably have noticed the law about shop hours being broken right and left. Many local authorities take a relaxed attitude to this, especially when the shop is staffed by the members of the owner's family. It is as well to find out your own local authority's stand, if you plan to stay open outside the prescribed hours.

A Private Member's Bill (called The Shops Bill) is at present before parliament. If it goes through, it will bring to an end the legal controls of shop opening hours as a result of growing pressure to see the law changed.

premises for a retail business

There is one common factor shared by almost all retail businesses: the need for a street frontage. Generally this means that the shopkeeper must find ready-built premises in a shopping centre (though if it is a new development, he may be the first occupier).

He needs to choose the right shop in the right location in the right district, and adapt it to his own needs.

choosing the district

It is doubtful whether anybody chooses an area in which to trade completely at random. You, too, will probably have reasons of your own for wishing to open a shop in one part of town rather than another.

By all means use your inclination as a starting point, but keep an open mind: if your investigations show that the preferred district is a no-hoper, look elsewhere.

Find out, preferably by personal investigation over a period of time, whether the area is prosperous or declining. Try to find out what the unemployment rate is: closed-down factories are an ominous sign, if there is an industrial area near by. Note 'For Sale' boards on private houses – if there are many, and they remain for a long time, there may be more people moving away from the area – or trying to – than are coming in. If there are many High Street shops for sale or rent, you will not have any trouble finding one, but you may not do much good there.

Look what other shopping centres there are near by. It may be that the more prosperous residents, the ones with cars, are accustomed to take their business farther away, perhaps to some big, new shopping complex, so that you would have to make do with the shoppers who cannot manage or afford the journey.

Do people come to work in the district? Look for offices, schools, colleges, industrial estates: people who have to shop in their lunch hour seldom go far afield. On the other hand, if you mostly sell to people who commute in, you may be twiddling your thumbs on satur-days, which elsewhere are the best shopping days.

Where there are any other reasons why people should come into the district – a swimming pool, a central library, council offices, a museum or art gallery – all these can bring in potential customers from other districts. If there is a railway station or bus terminus near by, the users may have to pass along the shopping street: good for business.

choosing the location

For a shop, nothing is more important than location: it must be where the customers go. For most, the more prominent the location, the better, because although much of the custom may come from regulars, a good deal comes from passers-by, who are lured to come in on impulse.

A small shop in a small suburban shopping parade probably enjoys little passing trade and may have a captive clientele of local residents, particularly the mothers of young families and the elderly. By staying open later than the High Street shops, it may attract working wives and people who have simply run out of something. If this is the sort of shop you want finding premises will be largely a question of locating a vacant property. But be careful about competition: there may not be enough trade for two butchers or two hardware merchants.

In a High Street shopping centre, the presence of a competing business may not necessarily be a disadvantage; it can even be a good thing, up to a point.

Where there are several shops of the same kind in a shopping district, it encourages people to travel there; customers like the prospect of choice, an alternative source near by: that source could be your shop. For some kinds of shop, competition is a positive factor: bookshops and shoe shops for instance. Book-buyers like to drift from shop to shop, browsing: a shoe customer will prefer to know that if the shoes she or he wants are not available in one shop, there is another shoe shop near by. Estate agents, too, gain a collective benefit from being closely associated with each other – people tend to visit a number of agencies, so there is no harm in making it easy for them.

A specialist shop, such as a builder's merchant, or a musical instrument shop, whose custom hardly depends on passing trade, may do well enough in a side street: it will attract specialist customers by becoming known in the trade.

Every shopping street has its 'dead end', where the trade is slower, and the shops are less prosperous and change hands more often. It is important to identify and shun this unlucky location (probably marked by a rash of For Sale and To Let boards).

Even in the 'live' part of the street, some locations can be better than others. If you are taking over a going concern, you have, obviously, less choice. But if you are buying or, more probably renting, vacant property to convert to your own use, give preference to one sited where people have to pause: next to a pedestrian crossing, a bus stop, near a parking place.

buying a going concern

If you decide to take over a shop which is at present trading, the first thing you will want to find out is the owner's reasons for selling. They may be genuinely personal – such as ill health, or retirement. Or they may be strategic: perhaps the owner has heard rumours of a huge new supermarket to be built nearby, or of a large local factory closing down, and is getting out while the going is good. Find out, if necessary by questions to the planning authorities, what new developments are planned in the area. A new main road bisecting a shopping district can halve its trade. Designating roads as one-way can be almost equally bad for trade, as it discourages some traffic from entering the area. A new hypermarket or shopping precinct could be fatal.

Or perhaps the present owner simply has not been able to make a success of the business, in which case the question is – can you? You should not only scrutinise the shop's accounts, but if possible also observe the proprietor at work. The reason for his poor financial performance may be idleness, incompetence, understocking or over-stocking, understaffing or overstaffing, poor choice of goods or of opening hours. Perhaps it is the location that is at fault, and no shop in that line of business could succeed there.

There are other considerations: if the fixtures and fittings are not to your likeing, how much will it cost to refit the shop? There may be no choice whether to buy or rent the premises. When renting, which is more common, you must know how long the lease has to run, whether it is renewable and on what terms. In a repairing lease, the consequent dilapidation liability must be allowed for in financial planning.

There is also the problem of what the goodwill is worth. A shop which is doing poorly cannot claim much of that, but even if it is doing well you cannot be sure that the customers are regulars who will transfer their custom to you.

You will, of course, have the property valued by a professional valuer and its leases and accounts throughly inspected, before coming to a decision.

starting a new business

You may be looking for an empty property in order to start a completely new shop. Where such a property is brand-new, in a newly built development, it may be difficult to assess your potential custom. But you should at least inspect the district; ideally, the development should include new housing or be near a residential area or a commuter area.

If you are thinking of taking over empty premises previously used as a shop, find out why the previous owner closed down: perhaps this one of those 'dead' sites where no business ever succeeds.

You will have to clear any change of use with the local authority's planning department. But if you intend to carry on a business of a similar character to the previous one, there is likely to be no problem. Most retail businesses are considered as interchangeable, and you can freely convert from one kind to another without permission. However, if you carry out any structural alterations to the building, your plans must be approved in the usual way.

You should consult your fire prevention officer for your own good, even if you think you do not come under any regulations. Some kinds of businesses, such as garages, which have special fire hazards, have of course, their own regulations.

accepting credit cards

If your goods carry a profit margin reasonably in excess of the credit card companies' commission (at present around 4 to 5 per cent), you may decide to try to attract more customers by becoming what is called a credit card agent.

When you have signed an agreement with the credit card company, you will be supplied with vouchers, a printer, and instructions how to use them. You may be given an envelope in which to send or hand the vouchers to the bank, or you can hand them over to cashier at the bank, as you would cash or cheques. Your account is immediately credited with the full amount on the slips, and the percentage due to the credit card company is direct-debited from your account to theirs. You receive a regular statement from the credit card company showing all the transactions, and the service charge or commission deducted.

Each retail outlet has a 'floor limit' which is the amount above which the retailer must telephone the credit card company for authorisation.

But credit card trading is not appropriate to some forms of retail trade, such as food shops or others where the margin of profit is low, because of the credit card company's service charge or commission. You must not charge the customers differently according to whether they pay by credit card or not, in order to recoup yourself for the commission.

having what it takes

Most people have idyllic childhood memories of playing shop: reality is quite a bit different.

It helps to be an early riser, especially in the food trade, such as a greengrocer who has to go to his wholesalers in the early hours, and be back in time to open the shop. Or there may be early-morning deliveries to attend to, as in the case of a newsagent. You may not get to bed very early either, because accounts, stock control, VAT, ordering, dealing with credit card business may all have to be dealt with in the evening.

The advice that you should acquire some working experience before setting up on your own applies doubly to shopkeeping, not only in order to learn some of the mechanics of the trade but to find out if you are temperamentally suited to it.

If your customers become irate, you will hear about it pretty soon. But no matter how you feel, you will have to appear unfailingly cheerful, patient, polite, and helpful even when customers offer a good deal of provocation. An offended customer is unlikely to return.

buying stocks

This is the heart of the matter for any shopkeeper: he invests a large proportion of his capital in his stock, and must buy it wisely.

symbol groups

Some shopkeepers, particularly in the grocery trade, take on the big battallions with their own weapons by joining a voluntary symbol group which is a retailers' buying organisation (such as VG, Spar, Mace, Wavy Line) in order to secure the large discounts that manufacturers offer to bulk-buyers.

The retailer agrees to take a certain amount of goods each week from the designated wholesaler for his area and receives better terms than he would get on his own, and possibly other advantages such as a fascia with the group's symbol and the shop's name, help with the layout and fixtures. In some cases, start-up help is given, the wholesaler may give the newcomer help in finding a shop and finance for it.

Details of the relevant wholesalers are listed geographically under 'symbol group' in the Grocer Marketing Directory (published by ▲ William Reed Ltd, 5–7 Southwark Street London SE1Y 1RQ (telephone: 01-407 6981), an expensive book, so ask if your reference library has it) or can be found through the trade press, mainly grocery, but also, for example, hardware. The applicant shopkeeper must offer some evidence of financial security, such as a bank reference. If he is already in business, the wholesaler will inspect the premises to see that they are in line with the organisation's requirements.

If there are other shops belonging to the particular symbol group in the neighbourhood, the wholesaler may refuse to take on another.

Members of the group must undertake to stock a certain number of the organisation's own-brand products, but are free to buy goods from agencies other than the designated wholesaler.

how much to stock

Some products deteriorate rapidly (flowers, bread, greengroceries);

others do not spoil with keeping, but go out of fashion (clothes, shoes). Even when they neither spoil nor date (most hardware), if nobody buys them, they bring in no profit with which to buy new stock, and take up the space needed for this stock. So in every case, a rapid turnover of stock is desirable. Stock unsold is cash tied up or lost.

Do not be tempted to over-stock, perhaps by an attractive quantity discount, nor to diversify too much.

The ideal is to buy only what your customers want, and to buy no more of it than you are able to sell.

You could buy through a symbol group, if you belong to one; or from a wholesaler; or from a cash-and-carry warehouse (a kind of retailers' supermarket); or directly from a manufacturer. They are not mutually exclusive. You might think that your orders are unlikely to be large enough to qualify for the quantity discounts which the manufacturer makes available to buying organisations and wholesalers, but do not dismiss the idea of buying direct from manufacturers.

buying direct or from wholesalers?

When you first open your shop, if you are in a price-competitive field, it is important to try to open with a bang, not a whimper. Your opening offers should be good, and as the initial stocking of the shop is likely to be your largest single stockbuying for a long time, you may qualify for a quantity discount on this order. This is also the time to establish contact with the representatives of the major firms (probably four to eight) whose products are likely to account for a large part of your turnover. The manufacturers' representatives will have a good idea of what are competitive retail prices for the particular products, and may help you to reach them by means of promotional allowances, that are extra discounts, or by providing redeemable coupons for customers.

Obviously, you must check that you are not overlooking other sources of supplies that are cheaper, by joining a symbol group and finding a good cash-and-carry source.

Plan your opening carefully: there is no second chance to make a good first impression. Choose about twenty top selling lines and be prepared for very low profit margins on these. They can be from a mixture of supply sources; choose the best items from each.

When stocking your shop initially, you may be able to negotiate extended credit from your supplier, perhaps no payment for two months, then one-sixth of your opening order to be paid for over the following six months.

An advantage of dealing direct with the manufacturer is that if there are damages, the reps have facilities for exchange or credit which a symbol group or cash-and-carry store may not afford to you. A keen rep can use these facilities to give the retailer a little extra discount on his purchases. You should be aware that damages eat into profit margins just as outdated stock does.

It is possible that manufacturers are less likely to run out of stock than a buying group – and lost sales lead to lost customers. But an advantage of indirect buying, if you stock many items, is cutting down on the time it takes to accept and check deliveries: much of your stock will arrive on one van, or, in the case of a cash-and-carry, be collected by you from one address. There will also be a considerable saving in paperwork.

what to stock?

There is, of course, no single answer to the question of which products and lines you ought to stock. It is partly common sense, partly flair, and partly experience – so here, too, it helps to have worked in the trade.

Customers hardly ever give prior notice of their wants, but expect to find what they want when they want it: and if it is not there in your shop, they go somewhere else, rather than wait for it to be ordered. So the shopkeeper must keep on his toes, trying not to run out of anything, especially the most popular lines.

This demands keeping proper records and a constant check on what goes out, plus efficient and far-sighted reordering, which takes account of the fact that manufacturers do not always meet delivery dates, and that wholesalers have been known to run out of some products.

You must store your stock in such a way that it deteriorates as little as possible and does not acquire that grubby, shopworn look which is so off-putting to customers.

You must rotate it, making sure that articles bought at the earliest period are put on sale first. Some food products are marked with 'sell by' dates, or shelf-life limits, and become unsaleable, once these dates are passed.

Goods which have failed to sell or have passed the peak of saleability should be marked down in price, or thrown away, if perishable. Apart from taking up space fruitlessly, they create a bad impression. You might hold a seasonal sale or sell off unwanted stock week by week, or even day by day, depending on the type of goods.

display

When you think of shops, you think of windows, their distinguishing feature. No other kind of business depends so much on visual display to attract customers.

What is essential is that the display should appear fresh, uncluttered and up-to-date: not dusty, crowded and superannuated. The window should be well-lit, as eye-catching as possible, and changed fairly often. If there is any item that you want to promote specially, it should have pride of place.

Prices should be clearly marked, whenever possible. Leaving off price tickets does not encourage people to come inside to ask the price: it makes them suspicious and puts them off.

If you decide to make your shop self-service, the goods must be easily accessible and each article marked with its price. And you must make sure that the checking-out will not create a bottleneck.

When you acquire a shop, the previous owner's fixtures and fitting may suit your purpose exactly, but it is more likely that you will want to make some changes, if only by redecorating. If you are changing the nature of the shop's trade, you will want to start from scratch.

Plan this carefully beforehand, making a list of your requirements and a provisional sketch of the layout; then get estimates from several firms of specialist shopfitters, choosing the one that offers the best value for money. Visit any relevant trade exhibitions such as Shopex which is held every June at Olympia, London, and concentrates on shopfitting, self-service and display equipment. Use your buying group facilities and choose the best that you can afford. Fittings have to last a long time and penny-pinching at the initial state might prove expensive latter.

coping with theft

A shopkeeper can be stolen from in various ways: by having his shop broken into, by pilferers on his own staff, by shoplifters (these last two are politely known as 'shrinkage').

shopbreaking

You cannot make your shop burglar-proof, but you can make it harder to burgle. Before you start trading, consult the crime prevention officer at your local police station, and perhaps get a good security firm to inspect the premises and install all necessary devices: locks and/or bolts on all doors and windows (not forgetting the basement and the attic); burglar alarms, not so sensitive that they go off all the time; and anything else that seems sensible. But make sure that what you do does not conflict with the fire prevention regulations.

Other precautions include great attention to locking up; every key accounted for at all times; a light left on all night. Do not leave money in the till overnight; leave it open at night – a thief would open it anyway, causing unnecessary damage (most insurance companies insist on this.) Do not have large sums of money in the shop at any time. Send someone to the bank with it. After banking hours, use the night safe.

You should have adequate insurance from the beginning of trading. If you do happen to be burgled, good stock control will pay off, as you will find it easier to list what has been stolen, which will help in getting your claim settled more promptly.

pilferage by staff

This can take the form of a hand in the till or stealing from stock. By and large, it is the bigger firms' problem: supermarkets have the highest rate of shrinkage. The small shop run by the owner and his family needs less internal protection. But there should be rules about employees' own purchases from the shop.

Although it is difficult to know who is trustworthy, you should be as discriminating as possible about whom you employ. Demand, and take up, references. It is a nerve racking business and not likely to improve relations with staff, having to practice eternal vigilance, constantly checking the deliveries, the stock, the till. Experience will teach you what precautions are necessary.

shoplifting

This is more of a problem if the shop has a self-service layout, or if the goods are displayed on stands or racks (as in many clothes shops). You will hardly be able to afford to employ a shop detective, but it might be worth while to consider renting a closed-circuit TV system; you will get back some of the cost in tax relief. Often the presence itself of such a system is a deterrent. Place the monitor screen so that it can also be seen by customers.

Strategically placed mirrors, perhaps convex ones, can help a lot, at modest cost. The shop itself should be well lit, with no murky corners, and shelves or racks of goods should have full light on them.

Expensive pocketable items, such as calculators, for example, can be chained to the stands: perhaps electrically connected so that a buzzer sounds if the chain is removed.

Advice on these and other anti-theft devices can be sought from a security firm specialising in shop protection.

Vigilance is essential, but however suspiciously a customer may be behaving, do not challenge him until he has removed an article from the premises. Only if theft has taken place, and you have good grounds of suspecting who did it, can you make a citizen's arrest of a shoplifter. if you 'arrest' someone and then he or she is acquitted, so that no theft has been proved to have taken place, the arrest would be unlawful and you could be made to pay heavy damages.

'dud' cheques

When you accept a cheque, there is always a possibility that it may bounce, unless you insist on the production of a cheque card, and write

its number down on the back of the cheque. This guarantees payment
if you took the cheque in good faith, and you can insist on the bank
paying up, to a set limit (at present £50) even if the chequebook and
card should turn out to have been stolen, or if the customer's account
is empty.

Do not accept any other identification, such as a driving licence, since
it does not guarantee the owner's solvency. Do not accept cheques for
more than the current £50 limit without checking with the customer's
bank, or holding up delivery of the goods until the cheque has been
cleared. Some shops are willing to take two or three cheques for single
purchases costing over the limit, but this invalidates the bank's guarantee of the cheque card, and possibly none of the part-payment
cheques would be honoured.

credit card fraud

The holders of credit cards such as Barclaycard, Access, American
Express, Diners Club, are supposed to notify the issuing organisation
as soon as they discover a card to have been lost or stolen. If you
accepted a stolen card in good faith, however, the issuing organisation
will pay you the money. The credit card company may send details of
stolen cards to shops which are likely to be at risk, with instructions
not to accept those cards. But it is difficult for a shop to check back
every single card that is offered.

learning the law

The shopkeeper must comply with a number of laws, both criminal
(such as the Weights and Measures Acts, the Food and Drugs Act)
and civil (such as Sale of Goods Act and Unfair Contract Terms Act),
which aim at enforcing fair trading, quite apart from the special rules
and regulations which apply to food and food hygiene. The intending
shopkeeper should make himself throughly familiar with them.

▲ The Consumers' Association's advisory service department, 14 Buckingham Street, London WC2N 6DS (telephone: 01-839 1222) runs
training courses for retailers on the subject of how the law affects
them, with special reference to sales and credit legislation.

Trade Descriptions Act

This act makes it a crime for a trader to describe any goods falsely, and to sell or offer for sale goods so misdescribed. It covers many things, including ads, display cards, oral descriptions, and applies to quantity and quality, that is, fitness for purpose of goods, and statements about prices. You must not name a price lower than some supposed earlier price ('now £4, reduced from £6.50') if the goods in question were not previously offered at the higher price for 28 consecutive days in the last six months. What you would have to do is display a disclaimer: a notice stating that they were not previously offered at a higher price.

This act is enforced by trading standards officers of the local authority, who have the right of entry to shop premises, and may seize goods if they suspect the law is being broken.

Weights and Measures Acts

This legislation, which includes numerous orders and regulations, also concerns itself with the truth of advertisements regarding price and quantity, and the giving of short weight (or measure) by a shopkeeper. It is also enforced by officers from the local authority's Trading Standards Department, who check scales and other weighing devices on trade premises, as a matter of routine and as spot checks.

Sale of Goods Act

This act has guided the relationship between seller and buyer for nearly a hundred years, and any one of its sixty-odd sections is likely to affect the retailer. Amongst other things, it sets out the implied conditions that are taken in law to obtain when a contract is made between a buyer and seller of goods. The most important one of these is that the goods should comply with their description and be fit for the purpose for which they are normally used. The contract of sale is made between the shopper and you, the retailer (not between the manufacturer and the shopper). So, the law places on the shopkeeper the onus of ensuring that the goods he sells are free from defects. If they are found to be defective, he must, strictly speaking, refund the money (in practice he may offer, instead, to replace the goods). Afterwards he can take the matter up with his supplier, being now himself the aggrieved party.

The Unfair Contract Terms Act is concerned, in part, with preventing or restricting a retailer from avoiding his business liability towards a customer. He must not write into the contract of sale any so-called exclusion clause which would restrict his responsibility and liability for any breach of legal duty towards the customer. This would include trying to get out of accepting liability for loss or damage of articles entrusted to you for servicing, or trying to exclude liability for the late delivery of goods that you had promised by a certain time, unless any such clauses could be shown to be reasonable.

worth getting and reading

A booklet *Fair Deal* prepared by the Office of Fair Trading is a shopper's guide to a number of relevant acts, practices, codes, and problems which are equally important to both sides of the shop counter. A leaflet on the *Law relating to the sale of goods* is available free from ▲ the Department of Trade, Gaywood House, 29 St. Peter Street, London SW1P 3LW.

Croner's Reference Book for Self-employed and the Smaller Business ▲ 173 Kingston Road, New Malden, Surrey KT3 3SS (telephone: 01-942 8966) includes explanatory notes on selected Acts of Parliament.

giving customers credit for goods or services

As a business person you are perfectly free to give credit to your customers for goods or services which you have supplied to them, that is, you can agree to allow them to defer their payment. However, if you make any charge for giving credit to customers you ought to be aware of how the law regulates credit agreements between business people and their customers.

Where a trader cannot, or does not want to, provide credit himself, he can refer those of his customers who wish to buy goods on credit terms to a credit agency (that is a body which provides credit facilities, such as a finance house). The finance house then buys the goods in question outright from the trader, and the customers enters into an agreement to buy those goods on credit terms from the finance house. In practice, the handing-over of the goods is from trader to customer.

The Consumer Credit Act 1974 regulates most of the agreements under which credit is advanced to any person (but not where credit is advanced to a company), regardless of whether the credit agreement is a hire purchase, a conditional sale or a credit agreement in respect of services rendered or goods supplied. It applies whether the person supplying the goods or services provides the credit facility himself or refers his customer to a credit agency or finance house.

The Act gives customers the right to require a written quotation, clearly stating the exact terms on which credit is on offer. If you cannot comply with this, because you lack certain information needed for a full credit quotation, you must provide an estimated credit quotation. You may inform the customer that credit will not be available to him (e.g. because of his low credit rating).

credit brokerage business

Any business which introduces individuals who want credit to other businesses offering such facilities is a 'credit brokerage' business. So, a shopkeeper who does not want to sell a TV set on credit terms, but refers his customer to a company which provides credit facilities, and then sells the TV set to that agency (which sells it to the customer on credit), is operating a credit brokerage business. If your business becomes such a credit brokerage business, you must have a category C licence from the Office of Fair Trading (OFT) (Consumer Credit Licensing Branch, Government Buildings, Bromyard Avenue, Acton, London W3 7BB.)

consumer credit business

Any business which provides credit under credit agreements which are regulated by the Consumer Credit Act is called a consumer credit business, for example, a shop selling goods on its own credit terms or a credit agency (finance house) which sells goods under hire-purchase agreements.

If your business is a consumer credit business, you will need to have a Category A Licence issued by the Office of Fair Trading unless the business is not a partnership or a company but is owned by an individual and does not grant credit exceeding £30.

The OFT will only grant a licence if it is satisfied that the person is a 'fit person' to carry on the type of business in question. There are severe penalties for unlicensed trading and agreements are unenforceable by the unlicensed business (but remain enforceable by the customer).

complications

If your business is a consumer credit business or a consumer brokerage business, you ought to be aware that the Act contains a large number of provisions, designed in the main to protect the interests of the customer, which are not due to come into force before 1984 (although some similar provisions apply already under the Hire Purchase Act and some other legislation).

Because consumer credit legislation is very intricate and involves many regulations and calculations, you should read carefully the information booklets, brochures and leaflets issued by the Office of Fair Trading which include *Credit Charges* (how to calculate the total charge of credit at the annual percentage rate of charge), *Advertisements and Quotations Regulations, Responsibilities of a Licensee, Low cost credit exemption, Regulated and exempt agreements* and many others, all ▲ available free of charge from Office of Fair Trading, Bromyard Avenue, Acton, London W3 7BB (telephone: 01-749 9151). The OFT will go on issuing free guidance material on various parts of the Consumer Credit Act as they come into force.

Some dreams explored

There are some businesses that have an enduring appeal for people hoping to become their own boss: having a bookshop; keeping a pub; being a newsagent. These seem to require no special training, and they bring you into contact with things which are generally associated with pleasure: alcoholic drink, magazines, tobacco, sweets, books.

An employment agency has the appeal of involving dealing with people, something which everybody believes themselves to have a natural flair for.

being a bookseller

Many middleclass, middleaged people have a fantasy of keeping a bookshop because they like the books themselves and the kind of people who buy books. What is more, they imagine that they will start off by selling, secondhand, all those surplus books now on their own shelves at home.

The reality is not so promising.

Even secondhand bookselling needs some expertise. You must learn what to charge to make your customers feel that they are getting a bargain, while you still make a profit, however modest.

Being aware of educational requirements may be useful, as students may come to your shop searching for cheaper copies of the set text. So you will want to find out what the current 'O' level and 'A' level texts are, especially in english, french and german literature; what texts are being used by local polytechnics, colleges of further education, and other institutions of learning.

For selling new books, publishers have set discount rates, and while quantity discounts vary from publisher to publisher, they all discourage small orders – a single copy of one book carries almost no discount. (You will have to decide whether it is worth stocking a large number of a particular book in order to get a higher discount, perhaps take a gamble that it will be a bestseller.) You must, nevertheless, be willing to order for a customer any book that you do not have in stock, without charge or in return for a small deposit. This is a condition of membership of the Booksellers' Association (154 Buckingham Palace Road, London SW1 (telephone: 01-730 8214).

A bookseller must belong to the Booksellers' Association, otherwise he would find it difficult to open an account with any publishers – that is, to buy his stock on credit.

The selling prices of new books are laid down by publishers and must be strictly observed. If you tried to sell more cheaply, the publishers would soon close your source of supply and you would have to rely on selling 'remainder' books. These can be bought from remaindered book merchants who buy them cheaply from publishers.

Apart from remaindered books, the exception to the strict resale price maintenance rule is the annual national book sale. Once a year, all booksellers then put into the sale any books that they have held for at least a year and never re-ordered. For these, a bookseller can charge what he likes. It is unlikely to make him rich.

keeping a pub

Not all publicans are self-employed, some are merely managers working for the brewery. To be self-employed, you must either own a free house or, more commonly, rent a public house from a brewery. For this, in the first place write to the brewery of your choice, ask for an interview and give details of yourself and your husband/wife, your experience in licensed trade (if any) and the amount of capital that you have readily available for investment in the pub. The available capital would have to be between £10,000 and £15,000 to buy the stock and necessary equipment.

Breweries are selective about tenants, and prefer married couples who will work as a team. You are unlikely to be considered if you are over 55 years old. It is an advantage to have worked in the trade and have had some specific training, apart from general knowledge of retail business. It is not enough to have been a devoted customer. Details ▲ of training courses may be obtained from the Brewers' Society, 42 Portman Square, London W1H 0BB (telephone: 01-486 4831).

A pub has to be licensed by the local justices and if you become its tenant you have to apply to be named as the licensee. The application goes to the magistrates who hold licensing sessions at irregular intervals, about 4 times a year, but a protection order can be granted to give temporary authority to carry on the business until a new licence is granted.

If your application to be a tenant is accepted by the brewery, you will be required to enter into an annual tenancy agreement which, amongst other things, requires you to sell only the brewer's beer and, where the brewer provides these, also wines, spirits, cider and minerals. Normally, if a tenant has reasonable demand for any brands which his brewer is unable or unwilling to supply, the tenant may buy them elsewhere. All the profits on the sales and any catering profit remain in your hands.

The work of a publican is hard and requires a capacity for appearing good humoured at all times, while keeping a sharp eye on both customers and any staff – short-changing or overcharging customers is bad for business in the long term, and giving friends double measures or cheap drinks is bad for business in the short term and long term.

luncheon vouchers

The publican has to make the most of any opportunities offered – providing food and anything else that may be required. If you want to accept Luncheon Vouchers, you have to make sure that they are used for food only, not drinks. The address of Luncheon Vouchers ▲ Limited is 50 Vauxhall Bridge Road, London SW1V 2RS (telephone: 01-834 6666). They will send you full details and display signs for your windows. Accepting Luncheon Vouchers does not cost you anything because they are redeemed at full face value. But you have to count them and take them or send them to the company for reimbursement.

being a newsagent, sweetseller, tobacconist

Running a small shop that sells mainly newspapers is not an easy life, nor outstandingly lucrative. Before you take over an existing shop, apart from the usual checks about the lease and the standing of the business, your must ensure that the wholesaler who is supplying the existing owner will continue to supply newspapers and magazines to you when you take over the shop. There is nothing automatic about this.

There may be a limitation on the numbers of papers that you are allowed to buy on sale or return, and some magazines are supplied on firm sale only. So you might find yourself with unsold stock on your hands.

You will need to stay open on every day on which newspapers appear, which is about 360 days of the year. Some newsagents, normally those who do not operate a delivery service, close on sundays, but this makes for lost sales.

You must be up before the lark every day, taking delivery of papers and sorting them and marking them up if you operate delivery rounds. Among your headaches will be sending out bills to tardy customers, explaining to customers why their newspaper or magazine has not arrived – which may be due to industrial action, at the publishers or wholesalers.

If you do home deliveries, you must find schoolchildren to do your rounds and will have to deal with the local education authority inspectors. There are by-laws about employing children to deliver newspapers; the children must be over 13 years old and you must be licensed by the local education authority and adhere to rules such as those about the weight of newspapers they may carry and that the rounds must be finished an hour before school starts. If you employ any adult, minimum wages are laid down by a wages council.

Sweets and tobacco being tempting, pocketable and anonymous, are readily stolen. Selling requires sharp-eyed vigilance both in the stock room and in the shop.

You will have to deal with numerous suppliers offering many lines, so that there will be the need for constant stock checks and reordering. This is where access to a computer might help, especially as the prices you are allowed to charge tend to change with surprising frequency virtually with every Budget.

It is not unusual for a newsagent to work a 90 hour week and do no better than just make a living.

combine it with a sub-post office?

If there is no sub-post office in the neighbourhood and you have suitable premises in which you could conduct the business if you where appointed, seek the support of the local population to arrange a petition. It would be a good idea to get the local authority interested in backing your application.

For a new sub-post office to be approved by the post office it must be at least one mile from any existing office in the case of a town, and two miles in the case of rural offices. Other considerations are whether the journey to the existing office is difficult (steep hills, muddy roads), whether public transport is good and primarily whether a poorly served area would benefit from a new sub-post office.

If you have an existing business, such as a shop, near a sub-post office and could accommodate it in your shop, you would have to wait until the sub-postmaster of the existing office resigned and the vacancy was advertised. Any person with suitable premises near the existing office can then ask for an application form and submit it to the head post master.

It is also possible to buy an existing sub-post office through an agent who specialises in the sale of sub-post offices. You would have to get on his mailing list first, and the agent will guide you through the stages of the purchase, but the final arbiter on appointing a new sub-post master is the post office.

Training is given in the range of services offered by the post office; it is a short course of about 44 hours.

A sub-post office obviously brings people into the shop and once they are there, they may well buy other things. One can make a living from a sub-post office, provided the overheads are reasonable. The salary is paid regularly, subject to review every three years. But – and there is the rub – you would again be an employee, and not starting your own business.

an employment agency

It is important to realise that an employment agency is not easy money, and needs people who are willing to face quite tedious work, have not only drive but also a vast amount of patience and a standard of education that enables them to deal with all types of people. It is important to have, or acquire, proper training in interviewing, backed by a good knowledge of office jobs (if this is an area in which you wish to operate).

Before starting an agency, consider what type of agency you intend to open – office agency or secretarial and clerical staff plus probably temporary staff in the same categories; or a specialist agency, for example computer staff, nursing staff, accountants, engineers. For specialists, it is important for at least one of the directors or partners to have a good knowledge and understanding of the types of jobs which occur in the particular area of work.

getting the clients

Building up contacts can be achieved by telephone or personal calls, or literature about your business. Calls are likely to be better because the initiative is then yours, not the client's.

A small agency must build up personal contacts and operate on a personal basis but this cannot be rushed, and immediate first-name familiarity on the part of the agency is not always the way in.

It is important always to tell your client the truth about prospective candidates and not to hard-sell the applicant, so that the client will have confidence in your opinions on candidates, and will trust you – which is vitally important. It is no good sending unsuitable applicants to clients in the hope of doing business.

recruiting the applicants

If your premises have a shop front, display the job vacancies for temporary and permanent staff in your windows. Alternatively, and in addition, it is a good idea to advertise permanent job vacancies in a local paper or, for London, a national paper. The wording of the advert should aim to bring in not a quantity, but the right quality, of applicants: the type of candidates who can do the job that is advertised. If you keep a record and analyse your responses from different media, you may learn which are the best to use for a particular type of vacancy. Advertising is costly: work out how much your incoming applicants are costing you.

money matters

If you have temporary workers, you will need a fair amount of capital because you pay the temporary staff straightaway at the end of each week (at an agreed fee per hour, tax and insurance deducted) and although the hourly charge to the client is more (by how much depends on the category of staff and whether it is a regular client) payment from the client will not come in for several weeks.

For permanent staff, you charge an introduction fee of 10–15 per cent of the annual salary. But when you first start an agency, the people whom you place in permanent jobs sometimes do not start their employment immediately, which can result in something like 6 to 8 weeks, or more, passing before you get paid any fees.

formalities

A licence has to be obtained from the Department of Employment before you start. You have to complete an application form with a lot of personal information including the work history of all partners or directors of the proposed agency. You have to display a notice which the Department of Employment lets you have, on the outside of the proposed offices and also put an advertisement with similar wording into the local papers, in case anybody wishes to raise any objection.

Until everything is cleared and a licence granted, it is illegal to carry on any business – so be careful not to sign any binding documents for the proposed offices, such as a lease. An outsider can raise objections to either the newspaper advertisement or the notice outside the proposed office, and if they are sustained by the Department, no licence is then granted.

Running an employment agency involves a great deal of record-keeping to comply with the Employment Agencies Act. There is probably enough record-keeping, paperwork and book keeping to keep one person fully occupied.

It is also important to have a good broad knowledge of the various statutes and regulations concerning employers and employees.

Advice and help may be obtained from the Federation of Personnel
▲ Services, 120 Baker Street, London W1 (telephone: 01-486 8264), and
▲ the Institute of Employment Consultants, 6 Welbeck Street, London W1 (telephone: 01-935 2631) which offers courses and sets examinations for membership.

An exporter

A manufacturer who sees little prospect of increasing his share of the home market may achieve the growth his business needs by selling his goods abroad, particulary to the so-called 'developing' countries. These not being highly industrialised, have to import many kinds of goods which they are not yet able to manufacture themselves. Being able to manufacture in larger batches may also make a manufacturer more competitive on the home market.

It is also possible to export without manufacturing, by setting up as an export merchant, and selling abroad goods bought from british manufacturers.

You must pick your markets intelligently, and do some basic research to find out which countries are most likely to want to import what you have to sell, rather than trying to export bacon-flavoured crisps to the middle east; or goods that are prohibited materials in another country according to their national regulations; or goods which do not comply with that country's standard specifications.

Selling abroad carries the same problems as the home trade – plus some others, such as: arranging the packing and shipment of goods to countries perhaps half a world away; complying with a great variety of foreign import regulations; securing payment in a world of shifting currency values. The exporter must be ready to cope with the unforeseen at home (such as a dock strike) and abroad (such as a revolution).

Exporting is not something you can fit into the odd moments you can spare from other concerns. If you plan to manufacture for sale both at home and abroad, either directly or through agents, you may need to have staff trained to deal with all aspects of exporting.

If your resources do not run to this, you will do better to entrust your foreign sales to an export merchant, while you are concentrating on building up the manufacturing side of your business. When this is on a firm footing, you can gradually build up your own export side.

There is yet another way to export: through buying-houses, or confirming houses, whose function it is to buy for foreign importers of British goods. They send out enquiries to a number of appropriate firms, and then place orders with those which offer the most favourable terms. It is the would-be exporter's job to make himself known to the appropriate buying-houses. You can get a list from the British Overseas Trade Board or the British Export Houses Association and make the first approaches yourself, as well as replying to all suitable enquiries.

If you plan to become an export merchant yourself, you will be wise to start with only one or two kinds of goods. Make yourself thoroughly familiar with them and do not extend your range until you are well established in that trade.

exporting, step by step

Most of the basic steps are the same whether you are dealing with goods manufactured by yourself or by some other firm.

First of all, there is the matter of language. English is an international language known in most parts of the world but if you are dealing with a country which does not have english as its first language or as one that is normally taught there, and you have to employ the services of a translator, make sure that he is technically knowledgeable if yours is a specialist market, so that you do not produce sales literature in the equivalent of quaintly phrased pidgin english. Operating instructions or manuals that accompany your goods should be in the local language, even if your business correspondence is carried out in english. It is useful to have a telex installed (to be ordered from British Telecom). Many foreign importers and british manufacturers now have telex, and this speeds up communications enormously.

finding your customers

You can obtain the addresses of prospective customers overseas through:

- The British Overseas Trade Board (BOTB) which usually has lists of foreign importers of almost all types of goods;
- Chambers of Commerce in the countries to which you intend to export. When requesting the information, be sure to indicate the type of goods you want to export;
- Chambers of Commerce in Britain;
- Directories of foreign importers, to be found in the commercial

section of most public libraries. They cannot be borrowed, but coin-operated photocopying machines are generally available);
- British banks which have branches overseas;
- Commercial attachés of the embassies or high commissions of the countries to which you want to export;
- Commercial attachés of british embassies abroad;

A personal visit to meet the customer may be worth the expense, even if you do your exporting through an agent.

Many small businesses use exhibitions overseas as a means of researching the market and meeting potential customers. The BOTB subsidises this under its 'joint venture' scheme in which ten or more firms have to participate.

making yourself known

When you have compiled a comprehensive list of prospective customers, start sending out publicity material. This should take the form of an illustrated leaflet describing the range of goods offered, accompanied by a circular letter which emphasises their good quality, and that competitive prices will be quoted on request. You should also mention that you can offer early delivery, and promise prompt attention to all enquiries and orders received. It would be tedious to type each letter individually, but a word processor bureau can personalise a circular letter by inserting each individual addressee's name and address.

Further mailings of circular letters should be sent at regular intervals, so that prospective customers are reminded of your existence. You might offer to send samples, where applicable, on request. But if they are valuable in themselves, it is wiser to ask for payment (in advance) for the samples.

the pro-forma invoice

If your circulars produce enquiries, or letters asking you to quote prices for specified quantities of your goods, these do not constitute orders. It is unlikely that anyone will place an order without first receiving a quotation. To save time, send this in the form of a pro-forma invoice – promptly and by airmail.

A pro-forma invoice looks like an ordinary invoice, except for the words 'pro-forma' in the heading. The figures you quote are binding. The invoice should indicate the type and quantity of goods, with details of their prices, the delivery time, the terms of payment (such as letter of credit or sight draft), the currency in which the deal is to be made, the method of packing. It should also state whether the prices quoted are:

f.a.s – free alongside ship
        price includes delivery to the docks

f.o.b. – free on board
        price includes delivery on board ship

c. & f. – cost and freight
        price includes freight charges, but not insurance charges, to an agreed port of destination

c.i.f. – cost, insurance, freight
        price includes both freight and insurance charges to an agreed port of destination.

All the terms should be clearly set out in the quotation or pro-forma invoice, because once the customer has signified his acceptance of this, it becomes a contract binding on both parties. If an order has been confirmed by the customer by telex, it is necessary to get confirmation by letter; pro-forma invoices must also be sent by mail.

dealing with suppliers

Unless you yourself are the manufacturer of the goods, or have them in stock, when you receive an enquiry, you will need to contact the manufacturers or stockists for quotations. You must emphasise that the goods will have to be suitably packed for export. The suppliers' quotations or pro-forma invoices should be with prices quoted f.o.b. or c. & f. or c.i.f., as requested by your customer.

If a supplier will only quote f.o.b., you must ask for an approximate shipping specification: the number of packages, cartons, cases, etc. that will be needed, the delivery time, their gross and net weights and their shipping measurements. You need this information to estimate the cost of freight, and insurance if required, plus the shipping expenses which the shipping agents will charge. Your suppliers' terms of payment may be cash with order or cash within seven days from receipt of invoice (possibly with a special cash discount); or monthly account (subject to satisfactory trade and bank references); or some other method of payment.

Be very meticulous in comparing your supplier's quotation with the pro-forma invoice you send to your potential customer overseas: any discrepancies between the supplier's descriptions and the customer's requirements must be sorted out because, once the order is placed, the customer will usually insist on receiving the goods exactly as specified in the pro-forma invoice. Any confusion about whether the prices quoted are f.o.b., c.&f. or c.i.f., can play havoc with the calculations of an exporter's expected profit.

Croner's Reference Book for Exporters contains a wealth of information about all aspects of the export trade, with separate entries for every country, giving a summary of its individual import regulations. It is a loose-leaf book, and its price (at present, £33.30) includes a year's updating amendments: the old page is removed and the new one inserted. The annual amendments subscription in subsequent years is (at present) £23.60.

arrangements for shipment

You will need the services of a shipping agent to book space on a ship bound for the port of destination. An efficient shipping agent is indispensable to the exporter: as well as attending to the actual forwarding of the goods, he will, if required, give help with shipping calculations and documentation.

It is to him and not to you that the goods should be consigned when they are sent to the docks for shipment overseas. If necessary, he will help you to estimate the cost of freight to any given destination.

The shipping agent nominates the ship to which the goods are to be sent, attends to all shipping details. When advised that the goods have gone forward to the ship, he will obtain bills of lading. These are detailed receipts for the goods, issued by the shipping company, containing a contract whereby the company undertakes to deliver the goods to a specified port of destination. The bill of lading is the most important part of the transaction: it is the document of title to the goods listed in it.

calculating your prices

In order to calculate the price to your customer abroad, you must have the following items of information:

- the amount of any discounts for cash or quantity that your supplier will allow you (unless you are exporting your own goods)
- cost of freight and shipping expenses; your shipping agent will calculate these for you
- bank charges; imposed by the bank through which you receive payment (between $\frac{1}{8}$ per cent and $\frac{1}{4}$ per cent of the total invoice value)
- insurance cost for c.i.f. quotations; you must also allow for the cost of insurance for the goods in transit from the works, factory or store in this country to the docks if this is not included in the supplier's price
- commission for your agent abroad, if you have one
- your own profit.

marine insurance

An exporter should arrange for a reputable insurance company to insure all his shipments. You will need to find a marine insurance company through an insurance broker. The insurers should supply you with a list of tariffs for different countries and types of risk. They will require information about each individual shipment, and will then quote accordingly. Some middle eastern countries have their own insurance companies, and therefore usually ask for the goods to be shipped c.& f. only.

A shipment is generally insured up to the moment it is claimed by the consignee, including any time spent in a warehouse overseas: but, because of the high risk of pilferage, insurance companies refuse to insure cargoes bound for some destinations, notably West Africa, beyond the moment when the cargo is discharged from the ship.

payment for exports

Commonly employed methods of payment are:

documentary letter of credit

With this method, the exporter receives payment from the bank within 7 to 10 days of presenting a complete set of shipping documents.

The customer, having accepted your quotation, opens a letter of credit in your favour: that is, he instructs his bank abroad to instruct a bank in Britain to pay you the agreed amount, on production of a correct and complete set of shipping documents (hence 'documentary').

There are several types of letter of credit (L/C for short). The most desirable is letter of credit confirmed by both the issuing bank and the advising bank in Britain. Payment is guaranteed in all circumstances – revolution, currency crash, act of God included. It is also the hardest to come by.

With a letter of credit confirmed by the issuing bank only, you should consult the advising bank in Britain whether the issuing bank is reliable in honouring its credits before you proceed. Any letter of credit not confirmed by either a british or a foreign bank should be regarded as worthless.

shipping documents

A complete set of shipping documents should consist of:
- the original letter of credit
- the exporter's commercial invoice, signed (not the pro-forma, although it contains the same information)
- the bill of lading: 2 originals, endorsed in the form demanded by the bank, signed, dated and stamped 'shipped on board' by the shipping company, plus 3 or more non-negotiable copies
- the insurance policy or certificate, in duplicate
- a set of two bills of exchange (which are a demand for payment)
- a certificate of origin, if required (issued and certified by the Chamber of Commerce) attesting that the goods are of UK origin and manufacture:

All these documents must conform in every particular to the requirements of the letter of credit and to the customer's order with regard to the type and quantity of the goods, the shipping marks (which identify the goods) and the shipping measurements of the packing cases.

If there are any discrepancies, the bank may withhold payment. And since the customer will be unable to claim the goods until the documents arrive at his end (forwarded by the bank), he may have to pay demurrage – the cost of storing them in a warehouse – for which he will want to be reimbursed by the exporter.

payment against sight draft

This method should be used only with a tried and proven customer. He, in turn, must trust the exporter to supply goods of the exact type and quantity ordered: he undertakes to pay on a specified date (usually the arrival of the shipping documents at the bank overseas or, in practice on the arrival of the vessel at the port of destination). The terms of payment should be specified. If goods are exported without an explicit arrangement to an unknown or unreliable customer, the exporter may find himself in a situation where he has lost control of the goods without any certainty of receiving payment.

The same shipping documents as for a letter of credit are required. The bank will release the shipping documents to the customer (thus enabling him to claim the goods) when it has collected the payment.

payment by 30, 60 or 90 days drafts

This is a method which grants credit to the customer. It should be extended only to known customers in good financial standing. Before the customer can claim the shipping documents, he must sign the drafts or bills of exchange, which you have issued, promising to pay the money due at some stated date – usually in 30, 60 or 90 days. The customer is then given the documents and can collect the goods – and sell them before having to pay for them.

Since you will receive your money with some delay, a reasonable allowance for interest should have been included in the price.

protection against export risks

The Export Credits Guarantee Department (ECGD), is a special government department designed to protect the exporter against some of the hazards of trading overseas. It provides a specialised form of credit insurance (a form of insurance not normally covered by other insurers) for the UK exporter.

Its policies cover insolvency, default, considerable transfer delays, new restrictions imposed on imports by the government of the country and other risks. Normally 90 to 95 per cent of any risk is covered.

Your application to the ECGD should include details of the type and volume of business, the kind of goods to be exported, the countries of destination. You will be given a general limit for the total amount of exports to be covered. The ECGD will then consider your individual applications for credit limits for particular customers overseas.

There are several types of ECGD policies: one operates from the date of contract, another, from the date of shipment, and a third covers the exporter from the date of manufacture of the goods until final payment is received. The premiums vary accordingly.

In the case of a claim, the exporter must submit photocopies of the contract signed by the defaulting customer, copies of the bill of lading and the export invoice, evidence from the collecting bank that the customer failed to pay even after several reminders; and copies of any correspondence with the customer about the non-payment.

exporting through confirming houses.

Some british export houses (confirming houses) act on behalf of overseas customers. Instead of dealing with the ultimate customer, the exporter deals with the confirming house, and presents the usual shipping documents to it. The ECGD will give insurance for such transactions if there is any giving of export credit involved.

Some confirming houses charge the exporter a small commission for their services, others are paid by the customer.

forwarding freight by air

The procedure is similar to that for shipping, with these differences: the goods are consigned to the airlines cargo depot at the airport, instead of the docks, and the document of title to the goods is called an air waybill, not bill of lading.

The British Export Houses Association and the Institute of Freight Forwarders will supply on request the names of freight forwarding agents, both for shipping and air freight.

exporting by air mail

If the goods you are exporting are neither bulky nor heavy, it may be preferable to send them by air parcel post direction to the customers. The procedure is simple: you complete the appropriate customs declaration forms (obtainable from the Post Office) and hand them in when posting the parcel in the usual way.

Every country has its own regulations as to customs declaration forms, packing and prohibited goods. All this information is contained in the *Post Office Guide* which can be consulted at any post office or brought for £1 from main post offices.

some useful addresses for exporters

▲ Association of British Chambers of Commerce, 212 Shaftesbury Avenue, London WC2 (telephone: 01-240 5830)

▲ British Export Houses Association, 69 Cannon Street, London EC4N 5AB (telephone: 01-248 4444)

▲ British Overseas Trade Board, 1 Victoria Street, London SW1H 0ET (telephone: 01-215 7877)

▲ Croner Publications, Croner House, 173 Kingston Road, New Malden, Surrey KT3 3SS (telephone: 01-942 8966)

▲ Export Credits Guarantee Department, Aldermanbury House, Aldermanbury Square, Aldermanbury, London EC2T 2EL (telephone: 01-606 6699)

▲ Fairs and Promotions Branch (BOTB), Hillgate House, 26 Old Bailey, London EC4M 7HU (telephone: 01-248 5757)

▲ Institute of Export, World Trade Centre, London E1 9AA (telephone: 01-488 4766)

▲ Institute of Freight Forwarders Ltd, Suffield House, 9 Paradise Road, Richmond, Surrey TW9 1SA (telephone: 01-948 3141)

Looking to the future

This book has been about starting a business. The question of making it expand, and even proliferate, would need another book to itself. But there are some things to consider when you begin looking ahead and making long-term plans.

changing the firm's status

If you started trading as a sole trader or partnership, you might consider, perhaps at the end of the first year, changing the status of your business to that of a private limited company.

The chief advantage of this would be to limit your liability (and your partner's liability, too, of course); it might also make it easier for you to raise finance. On the other hand, as the director of a limited company, you would not be able to set off your trading losses against income from other sources.

If you do decide on this move, make sure that you time it to your best advantage from the tax point of view, after consultation with your accountant.

delegating responsibility

If yours is a manufacturing business, even if you have started off by doing everything yourself, you will probably discover that you must save yourself for the more responsible aspects of your work and have someone else take over the more routine tasks. The next step might be to divide the major responsibilities with another person: one to concentrate on the technical side while the other one attends to the sales.

One possibility is taking on a partner or co-director with the qualifications you require, who would also be prepared to invest money in the business. This would bring a triple benefit: help in management, extra finance, and a newcomer with the incentive to work hard.

A personal recommendation from a knowledgeable person, such as your accountant, may be a way to find such a person; or by advertising in your trade press, clearly setting out your requirements, and what you have to offer.

Ask all applicants for personal and bank references (and take them up by personal contact with the referee). Agree a trial period with your chosen applicant, at the end of which either party will be entitled to call it a day if the arrangement is found to be unsatisfactory.

Before clinching the deal, agree with your new colleague the maximum amount that each of you will draw as salary, at least in the first year or two. It would be pointless to have a partner who insists on withdrawing his whole investment in the form of his first year's salary.

As your business grows, some of your original employees will be promoted to positions of greater responsibility. They will have become highly experienced in your business, they will know and may be known to your customers, so there is the risk that they might leave and set up on their own, perhaps even in the same area, taking away much of your business.

There is no complete protection against this – perhaps you yourself got your start in the same way? Nevertheless, when you promote an employee, and so revise his job description, you may be able to introduce some safeguards: a longer period of notice, for instance, and others which a lawyer might be able to suggest to you.

to expand or not?

Expansion means different things to different people. For the smallest firms, taking on one full-time employee may double the workforce, while for others who cannot get off the ground without a considerable staff, the notion of expansion is far more impressive. But in both cases the motivation is the same: greater profits.

One firm may seek to increase profits by trying for a greater turnover, with the existing range of products, another firm may look for ways to increase current profit margins, both confident that the demand for their product will continue. A third firm, having less confidence, will try to increase profits through developing new products within the same industry, or through diversifying into other, possibly unrelated industries.

Whichever way you choose, the same considerations apply as in starting up: you must plan ahead, time your actions accurately, and make sure well in advance that you have the necessary financial backing, and beware of overtrading. Many firms come to grief by attempting to expand in excess of their financial resources.

sub-contracting work

If in your case expansion means increasing your production, and your factory is already working to capacity, do not be in too much of a hurry to acquire new work space, plant and labour: you could be in serious trouble if there were to be a falling-off of trade. Instead, consider whether there is some part of your manufacturing process which could be turned over to a sub-contractor, which would ease the pressure of work, giving you time to plan what to do next.

If the part you want to sub-contract is a relatively simple operation, consider the possibility of handing it over to a youth training workshop or a sheltered workshop: there is bound to be one or more of each sort in your area.

A youth workshop is a government-sponsored scheme under the youth opportunities programme to train school-leavers in simple manufacturing processes. There are qualified instructors to ensure that the quality of the work meets the customers' specifications. Ask your local Department of Employment to help you in finding a suitable workshop.

A sheltered workshop is a similar institution, but catering for the physically or mentally disabled: many are privately sponsored. Your local authority should be able to help you find one.

In using such workshops, you are not only doing a social service, but perhaps training up future employees for your firm.

moving to larger premises

Think hard before taking on larger premises: additional space means additional overhead costs, and will inevitably increase your working capital requirements. Think whether you could manage with the space you have, through cleverer deployment of plant and equipment, or a more logical arrangement of the work sequence. It might be worthwhile calling in an expert on factory planning or work study, to advise you on this.

If you take on premises with room for growth, mark off the spare space and be ruthless about not allowing it to be used until the growth in production demands and justifies it. It is all too easy to fill up all available space with no compensating growth in turnover.

providing for retirement

In the early days of your firm, your mind will be busy with other things than providing for your old age, so it may not occur to you that you should already be thinking about making sure of an adequate pension. But if you wait till retirement is in sight, it may be too late to make provision: you had better start while there is plenty of time to go.

Since you, being self-employed, will qualify only for the basic state retirement pension, it will be necessary for you to have your own pension scheme. You will be doing yourself a favour in more ways than one. The contributions you pay towards your own pension qualify for tax relief at the highest rate of income tax that you are paying. As you come to pay income tax at increasingly higher rates (you hope!), your tax relief will increase correspondingly.

A pension scheme can cost very little, but if you feel the money could be put to better use in your business, some insurance companies offer pension plans with a 'loanback' facility; you can borrow up to the whole value of the policy, provided that you can offer acceptable security (other than the policy) and keep up the interest payments. You repay the capital when you retire (which may use up all the benefit you get from the policy). In fact, the loanback facility ought to be used as a last resort, if your business just cannot manage without the money – but you should be able to get a cheaper loan elsewhere.

There is a limit to the proportion of your net earnings that you can put into a pension fund. At present it is $17\frac{1}{2}$ per cent (it is even higher for people born before 1933, to enable them to make up for lost time). You can start taking benefits when you are 60 and before you turn 75, unless you have to retire early for health reasons.

what kind of provision?

There are a number of different pension schemes offered by insurance companies and unit trust investment firms (not all with full tax relief, though). Between them they offer a large number of choices and benefits, such as: the personal pension plan with or without profits; the unit-linked pension; the endowment policy; term assurance (which, being life insurance, provides for one's dependants rather than oneself). You can take out a policy with a single premium or with a premium which can vary from nothing to some high amount from year to year. You can subscribe to more than one scheme (provided you do not exceed the permitted ceiling); you will not be able to take your retirement benefit as cash, some will have to be in the form of an annuity; you need not buy it from the original company, if another one offers you a better deal.

The whole subject is so complex and mutable, that any treatment of it here would be superficial and misleading.

. . . a last thought

Every so often – say once a month – stop thinking about the day to day problems and consider what you are really trying to achieve: what you have already achieved so far and what needs doing to get you to your next goal. You have a better chance of arriving if you know your destination beforehand.

Index

Consumer Publications

The list of CA's Consumer Publications includes:

Avoiding back trouble

Avoiding heart trouble

Central heating

Cutting your cost of living

Dealing with household emergencies

Earning money at home

Getting a new job

Living through middle age

Living with stress

Making the most of your freezer

On getting divorced (England and Wales)

Pregnancy month by month

Raising the money to buy your home

Securing your home

The legal side of buying a house (England and Wales)

The newborn baby

What to do when someone dies

Where to live after retirement

Which? 25 years on

Which? way to buy, sell and move house

Which? way to slim

Wills and probate (England and Wales)

CONSUMER PUBLICATIONS are available from Consumers' Association, Caxton Hill, Hertford SG13 7LZ and from booksellers.